"Living in the twenty-first century means continually confronting fear and anxiety. If the Pentagon and the World Trade Towers are not safe, what is? Ex-Army Ranger Chuck Holton addresses these fears head-on in this honest and well-timed book. He reminds believers that our lives are in the hands of a sovereign God, and until He calls us home, we are indeed bulletproof."

—DR. AL MEREDITH
Senior Pastor, Wedgwood Baptist Church
Fort Worth, Texas

"My friend Chuck Holton is a man of character and perspective. He writes skillfully and with faith-grounded insight. We live in a time when courage is often celebrated but seldom practiced. We need to learn to trust Christ for our immediate futures as much as we must trust Him for our eternal futures. I pray God will use Chuck's book to release people from their fears and light a fire of Christian courage."

—RANDY ALCORN
Author of *Deadline* and *Heaven*

"This book is filled with riveting stories that impart life-changing spiritual principles. Chuck does a masterful job of drawing the reader into the life and experience of an Army Ranger, while at the same time communicating a call to passionate and sincere Christian living."

—DALE O'SHIELDS
Pastor, Church of the Redeemer
Gaithersburg, Maryland

BULLET PROOF

CHUCK HOLTON

Multnomah Books

BULLETPROOF
published by Multnomah Books
© 2005 by Charles W. Holton
International Standard Book Number: 978-1-59052-398-8

Cover image by Eric Long
Interior design and typeset by Katherine Lloyd, The DESK

Unless otherwise indicated, Scripture quotations are from:
The Holy Bible, New International Version © 1973, 1984
by International Bible Society, used by permission
of Zondervan Publishing House.

Other Scripture quotations are from:
The Amplified Bible (AMP) © 1965, 1987
by Zondervan Publishing House.
The Message by Eugene H. Peterson, Copyright © 1993, 1994, 1995, 1996,
2000. Used by permission of NavPress Publishing Group. All rights reserved.

Published in the United States by WaterBrook Multnomah,
an imprint of the Crown Publishing Group,
a division of Random House Inc., New York.

For information:
MULTNOMAH BOOKS
12265 Oracle Boulevard, Suite 200 • Colorado Springs, CO 80921

Library of Congress Cataloging-in-Publication Data
Holton, Chuck.
Bulletproof / Chuck Holton.
    p. cm.
ISBN 1-59052-398-9
1. Providence and government of God. 2. Christian life. 3. Miracles.
I. Title: Bullet proof. II. Title.
BT135.H64 2005
248.4--dc22
                                                    2004029217
10—10 9 8 7 6 5

"My father is all that becomes a man.
And I stand in awe."

From my journal
November 23, 1986
Age 16

★ ★ ★

This book is dedicated to you, Dad.
I love you.

CONTENTS

PART I

COMBAT ZONE

★ ★ ★

INVINCIBLE

Midnight,

somewhere in the Gulf of Mexico

A light rain pelted the USS *Guadalcanal* as it turned into the wind twenty-five miles off the coast of the Florida panhandle. Five MH-60 Black Hawk helicopters spun up for takeoff, the prop wash transforming the drizzle into a cold spray that caused miniature waterspouts to dance along the pitching, dimly lit deck. Seemingly oblivious to the ship's movement, seamen in color-coded helmets scurried about, making final preparations for mission launch.

I had just climbed aboard chopper three and was sitting on an ammo box with my back to the door gunner, who manned one of the two 7.62 mm Vulcan cannons situated behind the pilot on the special-ops-modified aircraft. These were the same Night Stalker crews we had flown with in Panama a year earlier, and the little stick figures painted in front of the guns on each chopper bore silent testimony to the action they had seen there.

Through the open door, I could see another chopper fifty feet away; I glimpsed a line of soldiers in black helmets hurrying out to it, each heavily laden with every sort of high-speed military hardware imaginable. As far as I could tell, none of it was standard issue. These guys weren't Rangers, like the rest of us, though some of them had been before they were "selected" for the ultrasecret unit they were now a part of. We affectionately called them "long hairs" because they all had long hair. (Not a very creative name, I suppose.) We weren't supposed to talk to them, but their impressive array of custom-made weapons and anonymous uniforms ensured that we talked about little else. They were the main event on this mission; we Rangers were only on board to provide support and security.

I looked over at two of the privates on my team—Lavoie and Urban—sitting with their feet dangling from the aircraft's open door. They were going to have a cold ride. Like me, they couldn't wait to get on with the show, mostly because we were all sick of being stuck on this ship. The last three days had been enough to make all of us glad we hadn't joined the Navy. We had been assigned bunks that stacked five high, with only about eighteen inches of space between each rack. And if the pitching and yawing of the ship weren't enough to make a guy sick, every couple of hours some purple-shirted Navy guys called "grapes" showed up in our quarters to check the levels on the ship's fuel tanks—filling the room with diesel fumes.

I finally ended up sleeping in the ship's fo'c'sle (forecastle), a large room all the way forward that had been set up as a workout area. Did I say sleeping? I actually spent several hours hanging my head out the anchor chain hole, gasping for some fresh air. How anybody could spend six months on a ship without becoming suicidal was beyond me.

A tap on the shoulder interrupted my thoughts. The door gunner was holding up an index finger. One minute to launch. *Let's get on with it!* I thought. I turned to watch the pilots running through their last-minute checks. Noting my interest, the gunner handed me an extra set of headphones so I could hear what they were saying. Not that I understood any of it.

"N2—103 percent."

"Check."

"Auxiliary pitot heat, off."

"Check."

The crew chief smiled at me from under his goggles and twirled his finger in the air. Translation: *Game on.*

The pitch of the Black Hawk's engines changed, its powerful turbine whining as if it couldn't wait to get off the ground. Then the five helicopters lifted off as one and the heaving deck of the carrier dropped away beneath us. G-forces pressed me into my seat as the nose of the chopper pitched forward and we picked up speed.

I clutched my M203 grenade launcher, held barrel down like we'd been trained. It was always a good idea. That way, in the unlikely event of an accidental discharge, nothing important—like the engine—would be damaged. This time, we were all carrying live rounds. This mission was the final test—the culmination of the last month of training which, if successful, would get us the green light to do this thing for real, on the ground in Iraqi-occupied Kuwait.

I looked out the open door of the helicopter as we hurtled over white-capped waves 250 feet below. The water looked cold, almost evil. I shivered.

Hard-rock music came blasting through my headset. My head jerked around in time to see the gunner finish connecting a wire from the onboard radio to the headphone jack on his Walkman. He grinned and gave me a thumbs-up. Background music. *Special-ops pilots. These guys are fun.*

A month ago I'd been enjoying one of the best deployments of my life—an entire summer assignment as an instructor at the United States Military Academy at West Point. Every year the Rangers were tasked to provide some noncommissioned officers to teach infantry tactics to the "yearlings," or first-year students. It was awesome. We got treated like superstars, because the cadets are taught to have great respect for NCOs. But it was more than that. The Rangers had just returned from the first major combat operation in nearly a decade, sporting combat jump stars on our uniforms—which were so rare we constantly got asked, "What is that little gold star on your jump wings?" Life was good.

Then Saddam Hussein invaded Kuwait. The next day, a camouflage Humvee drove up to our patrol base in the woods around Camp Buckner, and a West Point major stepped out with a message for us. The note said simply, "RETURN TO BENNING IMMEDIATELY." It had been sent by our company commander.

Twenty-four hours later, after an all-night road trip, we rolled up to the Ranger barracks on Fort Benning's main post. The compound boiled with activity—Rangers hurrying to inspect and palletize everything we would need for an

BULLETPROOF

extended deployment. I was struck by the practiced precision of it all. And this time I understood what enabled us to react so quickly. As a private, I had hated all of the inspecting, packing, unpacking, and repacking that we did in training. But now that I'd seen combat in Panama, I understood the importance of training on the tedious things.

They separated our battalion into "assault packages," pairing groups of us up with other special-ops units to accomplish the various missions our leadership had been given. My company had been tasked with protecting the exterior of the U.S. embassy in Kuwait City—at that very moment surrounded by thousands of Iraqi troops. Once we secured the exterior, the long hairs would go inside and get our people out.

A full-scale plywood mock-up of the embassy had been constructed on a remote section of an air force base in Florida. Meanwhile, our unit scrambled to learn how to execute our part of the mission. We started by laying out engineer tape on the dewy grass of our PT field, representing the dimensions of the embassy. Then it was just a matter of walking through our mission again and again until each of us knew exactly what to do.

After being flown to the USS *Guadalcanal*, we began practicing the operation in earnest. In conjunction with naval elements, air assets, and long hairs, we hit the mock-up on the beach over and over again, working out the kinks in the mission. I had to keep reminding my guys not to run in front of the miniguns when they exited the chopper. When it came time to use live rounds, a misstep could get a guy cut in half by four-thousand-rounds-per-minute of ball ammunition.

After three days and six dry runs, someone decided we were ready to try it with live ammo. This was the final test, and if we passed, it was likely that the order to execute the mission would soon follow.

This would be altogether different from our deployment in Panama. In Operation Just Cause, we had parachuted in with overwhelming force and, after the first twenty-four hours, spent the majority of our time watching people surrender. If this mission went off, we'd be fighting for our lives against a numerically superior force, dependent as much on combat support from the air as we were on our own trigger fingers.

This mission was "hit and git": Rescue the hostages and disappear before the enemy could get organized enough to resist us. The goal was ten minutes, max. If something happened and we were on the ground longer than that, things would get downright unfriendly, and fast.

Something in the back of my mind was less enthusiastic about this thrust into the Middle East than I had been about going into Panama. Maybe it was because I knew this action would be more difficult. Then again, maybe those combat images of losing buddies the previous year were fresh enough in my mind to keep me from wanting to go through it again.

Really, it didn't matter either way. I had learned to compartmentalize my feelings away and concentrate on my part of the mission. My men were counting on me to guide them through the operation successfully. If I got distracted, it wouldn't affect just me but my squad as well, and perhaps the entire mission. I wasn't going to waste time worrying about the outcome; I had to focus on performing my part.

I had learned to trust our commanders. In Panama, we'd been given the task of taking over a penitentiary that held political prisoners. Before we even boarded the choppers, however, word came down that our regimental commander, Col. William F. "Buck" Kernan, had actually called the prison on the telephone and informed them we were coming. *What?* We couldn't believe it. I sincerely believed he had just signed our death warrant by giving up the element of surprise. None of us could understand what would possess him to take such a risk. When we arrived at the prison, however, we were met by a neat line of unarmed guards standing out front, waiting to surrender. We accomplished the mission without firing a shot. Our commander had known what he was doing.

This time around, I worried about how seventy Rangers were supposed to hold off thousands of enraged Iraqis. I had to remind myself that it wasn't my job to understand; it was my job to carry out the mission I'd been given.

Civilian friends of mine couldn't understand that mindset and might have said I was foolish or even brainwashed to put myself into a situation like this. But because I trusted my commander, I found great freedom in ceding control of my well-being to him. Could it be I wouldn't come back from this one? Sure. But I could just as easily get run off the road into a bridge abutment on my way to a nine-to-five job somewhere in suburbia. All things considered, I preferred the uncertainty and risk of this life to the stale comfort of a more predictable and safe existence. And even though this mission scared me a bit, my guys needed me. No way would I let them go off into combat alone.

The helicopter suddenly dropped like a stone toward the black sea below, jolting me back to the present. For a split second I was weightless, free-falling toward the water and clutching for something to hold onto before my safety line caught and pulled me back down into the seat. I held on as the chopper dove to within thirty feet of the waves on its final approach to the beachfront landing zone in front of the embassy mock-up.

"One minute!" The crew chief gestured into the mass of bodies packed into the Black Hawk's dark interior. Only a few saw him, but they quickly passed it along to the rest of the men. My guys looked to me for their cue to "go hot"— to load their weapons with live ammunition. Pulling a magazine from my vest, I tapped it against my Kevlar helmet, then pushed it deftly into the receiver on my M203. Lavoie and Urban did the same, and I was gratified by the fluidity with which they charged their own weapons. All those end- less hours of disassembling and reassembling their M203s in training were paying dividends tonight.

We thundered over a Zodiac inflatable boat full of commandos—presumably Navy SEALs—as they headed for the beach, practically invisible but for the wake left by the boat. Then I checked my weapon's safety catch, making sure it was on, and started to finger the snaplink connected to my safety line.

The objective was clearly visible at this point. Smoke rose in columns from around the perimeter of the plywood fence surrounding the pretend embassy. The choppers began to decelerate, their tails flaring downward. Just when everything felt like it should be moving the fastest, time seemed to slow.

Time to focus. Time to go.

Just before touchdown, the door gunners opened up, hosing down the objective with a vicious belch of hot lead, chewing up the sand, as the rotor wash caused a momentary brownout. Settling on the beach just long enough for the men inside to scramble out and hit the prone, the aircraft lifted off scant seconds later. Once the dust began to settle, we could make out the dim shapes of bunkers around the outside wall of the embassy, and silhouettes of plastic "enemy" soldiers inside. I pumped a 40 mm training grenade into the nearest bunker, as Lavoie laid on the trigger of his squad automatic weapon on my left. The rattle of his gun was accompanied by the sound of rounds impacting the target.

Just then, something whooshed by over my head, and a split second later the bunker twenty feet in front of me evaporated with a flash. The shock wave from the explosion felt like a pro wrestler jumping on my flak vest. I buried my face in the sand as shrapnel and clods of dirt sailed through the air above me. *Wow! That was a 2.75 inch rocket!* I glanced at the sky behind me in time to see the Night Stalker Little Bird that had fired the rockets swoop down low toward the objective, spouting flame from its 5.56 mm miniguns as it passed. The knowledge that the pilots aimed their weapons systems by making a mark with a grease pencil on the windscreen wasn't especially comforting, as their rounds were impacting fairly close to my position.

No sooner had this thought crossed my mind than I heard Lavoie suddenly cry out, and I looked over to see him writhing on the ground in pain. *Oh no!* Rising to my hands and knees, I scrambled to his side, fearing he'd been hit by a stray round. I yelled, "Are you hit?" and was met by a stream of profanity as he continued to roll on the ground. It looked like he was trying to get out of his flak vest. "Brass!" he screamed. "Hot brass down my back!"

Then I realized what had happened. The passing chopper had been firing, ejecting hot brass cartridges, and one of them had dropped down the back of Lavoie's shirt. I quickly put my knee on his back, reached into his shirt, located the spent cartridge, and removed it.

Lavoie let out a groan. "Thanks, Sergeant."

"You scared me," I replied. "Now let's move."

Bounding up to the edge of the wall surrounding the embassy, we took our position at the southeast corner. I keyed the radio mic attached to my body armor and reported to the commander.

"Yellow three, clear."

"Roger, Yellow three. Hold what you've got. Out."

My team and I pulled security toward empty dunes of sand, trying to imagine what it would be like when we did this mission for real. Our briefing had shown that the real embassy in downtown Kuwait City was surrounded by buildings. The plan was to flatten them to disrupt the enemy, so we'd probably be looking at smoking rubble if this were the real thing. But for now, the rain had moved away and a moonlit sky showed a huge special-ops Pave Low helicopter approaching from the sea. The long hairs were inbound to extract our precious cargo.

While my men stayed prone, surveying their sectors of fire, I took a knee and thought about how tough it would be to lose any of them. These men were the brothers I'd always wanted as a boy. We'd been through a lot together. I wouldn't let anything hurt them, if I had to kill the whole city or die trying. I imagined having to hold off hundreds of Iraqi troops from this exposed position, protecting fellow Americans whom we'd probably never even see.

Looking through my night vision goggles at the empty dunes to my front, images of a fight to the death flashed through my head. For one moment, the real weight of the commitment I'd made nearly four years earlier to "support and defend" came looking back at me through that night scope. I realized fully, maybe for the first time, that I'd agreed to go to my death if that's what it took. I'd freely given up any choice in the matter. If my commander decided it was necessary to send me on a suicide mission, I had pledged to go.

Oddly enough, that thought didn't bother me much. In fact, it brought a sense of purpose and quiet determination. I wasn't in any hurry to get killed, but it felt good to be a part of something that transcended my own life.

Four minutes later, after the Pave Low had come and gone, the Black Hawks swooped back in from the sea and landed on the beach, their rotor blades phosphorescing with static electricity. We waited for a cue from our leader, then pulled back toward the choppers. Before we clambered aboard, I pulled out a small mag light and made sure each man cleared his weapon.

As the aircraft turned back toward the ship, I checked my watch. The entire mission had gone like clockwork. It had taken less than six minutes.

We were ready.

The confidence brought on by that knowledge made me

feel, well, invincible. I was armed with a belief in the mission, a knowledge that I was prepared for it, and the understanding that other competent men were watching my back. The risks were very real, but there were Americans out there who needed our help, and we weren't going to let them down. I suddenly felt as if I'd found the very wellspring of courage.

I felt bulletproof.

★ ★ ★

ONE

SPIRIT WARRIORS

29 January 2004
Mosul, Iraq

Something's wrong with this picture.

Jeff could see the barricade up ahead. It looked like road construction. Fifty-five-gallon drums blocked the road and Iraqi workers swept the pavement, while vehicles trying to get through were detoured onto a side street. Jeff saw the lead vehicle in their convoy—a gray Suburban—turn the corner and then stop at the roadblock. The vehicle he was driving was close behind.

I don't like the looks of this.

No sooner had the thought formed in his mind than automatic gunfire erupted from everywhere. The *pop-pop-popping* was so loud in his left ear that he was sure the gunman was right outside his window. He flinched instinctively at the sound and watched in horror as gunmen peppered the Suburban with bullets right before his eyes.

NO!

One of the first rounds smashed through the back window of the Suburban, pierced the driver's headrest, and struck the driver in the back of the neck. Another round penetrated the back door and the rear seat and struck a passenger in the spine. Still more bullets pierced the door frame next to Maj. Steve Ward, who was riding shotgun. Then a spiderweb of cracks appeared from bullets smashing through the windshield in front of him.

Jeff saw the Suburban hesitate for a moment, then bolt to the left, jumping the curb and plowing through the barricade as it tore out of the kill zone. Jeff hit the accelerator and followed suit, knocking more barrels aside, as the soldier riding shotgun in his vehicle attempted to return fire.

Once away from the congestion it became clear there had been no road construction. The ambush had been well planned and executed. As Jeff realized the full magnitude of what had just happened, he became very concerned for the three people in the lead vehicle, all of whom had become good friends in the time they'd been together in Iraq.

He picked up his radio and called the Suburban. "Is everyone all right up there?"

"We have a hit!" the major's voice crackled over the airwaves. "We have a hit! We're heading back to base!"

D-Main Base, Mosul,
thirty minutes earlier

The five warriors stopped everything and stood together. It was time to put on their body armor.

While their mission was one of peace, they were entering

a city at war. They knew the risks but also held a deep under-standing of their purpose in that place. With eyes closed, they stood in a circle and called on their Commander for safety, courage, and clarity on this mission.

As members of the U.S. Army Corps of Engineers, their specialty was construction, not destruction, so the military didn't consider them soldiers. But even though the military part of the campaign had been over for months, a greater fight still raged—a spiritual battle between chaos and order, turmoil and peace, discord and harmony. In this war, these five were frontline combat troops.

Norm would drive the Suburban, the lead vehicle in their convoy. He was a big Norwegian whom everyone called "Stormy" or "Bubba." That day, he had lent his extra-large body armor to a friend, which left him to go without. The thought didn't bother him; he knew that his safety in Mosul had much less to do with his bulletproof vest than it did with his standing before God. As the team prepared to leave, how-ever, someone came up to Norm and offered him an XL vest, which he happily accepted.

Gayle, a reporter for the Armed Forces Network, would accompany the engineers on their mission today, riding in the backseat of the lead vehicle. She wore a bulletproof vest, but it was only rated to stop nine-millimeter rounds.

Jeff, the driver of the second vehicle, went by the call sign "FM." It stood for "Family Man," because of the loving wife and two young daughters who awaited him at home. It had been a tough decision to come to Iraq, but he felt called to do so. Today was especially difficult for him, because it was his ninth wedding anniversary.

Their mission this day was to visit a local radio station and work up a report on what it would take to make the station operational.

After their short prayer, the team loaded up, with some armed Gurkha soldiers riding along for protection.

They left the main gate…and drove straight into the ambush.

Twenty minutes later, the convoy burst back through the gate of the compound, stopping in front of the aid station. Jeff watched anxiously as Norm stumbled out of the Suburban, holding his neck. Apparently he had driven the entire way like that—steering and honking the horn with one hand, while keeping pressure on a neck wound with the other.

A quick examination revealed that the bullet had deflected off the seat post behind Norm and wrapped itself up in the Kevlar collar of his flak vest, grazing off to one side. The round pierced both his uniform collar and his T-shirt collar but left only a scratch on his neck.

Quickly, the medics turned their attention to Gayle. The bullet had struck very close to her spine, but a closer look revealed that the vest had stopped the AK-47 bullet, even though it wasn't rated for such a powerful round. A hole in the shoulder of her vest showed that another round had gone straight through it—missing her body. Gayle had a nice bruise but was back on duty later that day.

Major Ward had only superficial injuries, despite being surrounded by bullet holes. In fact, a close examination of the lead vehicle showed that rounds penetrated every headrest, shattered both front and rear windshields, and riddled the door frames next to where people were sitting. Jeff's vehicle, despite being directly in the line of fire and only five yards or so behind the Suburban, was hit only three times, though it was clear the shooters had been targeting the driver's side.

As the team took stock of the damaged vehicles, it became obvious to everyone that they were looking at a miracle. The prayers offered up before they left had been answered in a big way. God had sent unseen protectors to ride with them on this mission.

RECKLESS LOVE

Don't get too enchanted with the miraculous deliverance Jeff and his friends experienced that day. Yes, it was certainly something for which to praise and thank God. But we are surrounded by miracles every day. What should impact us most about this story is not that the members of this team were shielded from harm in a dark and evil place, but that this band of Christian soldiers did not let the prospect of violent death deter them from God's calling on their lives.

It's a point that would have been just as valid if every one of them had been killed. In fact, not three months after this incident, four Southern Baptist missionaries were shot to death in a similar incident in the very same city.

Larry and Jean Elliott, along with David and Carrie McDonnall and Karen Watson, were on their way to a site in Mosul where they were planning a water purification project to bring fresh water to the people of the city. In an ambush almost exactly like the one just described, gunmen opened fire on their vehicle. Carrie McDonnall was the only survivor.

Career missionaries, the Elliotts understood the risks associated with being in Iraq. And they went anyway.

Their purpose was never to badger the residents of the predominantly Muslim country, but to preach the gospel with their *actions*, giving fresh water to anyone who needed it. Their greater goal, however, was to share living water with those willing to listen.

Some might say that being killed ended the Elliotts' chance to change people's lives. But in actuality, their death has leveraged their effectiveness, enabling them to inspire more people into His service. Before this incident, very few people knew about the exploits of this small band of committed believers. But in death, their story has been spread around the world.

Norma Martinez de Robbins attended the service in Bullock, North Carolina, to honor the Elliotts' lives of service. She says that the Elliotts' death has sparked a renewed fervor in her own life: "Now I'm more encouraged to tell and be faithful. They taught me loving is the first key to start evangelizing."[1]

The Elliotts were simply following the example modeled for them by Christ Himself. Speaking of His own pending crucifixion, Jesus said:

> "Listen carefully: Unless a grain of wheat is buried in the ground, dead to the world, it is never any more than a grain of wheat. But if it is buried, it sprouts and reproduces itself many times over. In the same way, anyone who holds on to life just as it is destroys that life. But if you let it go, reckless in

your love, you'll have it forever, real and eternal."
(John 12:24–25, *The Message*)

Reckless love. What better way is there to describe the actions of these intrepid missionaries? Oh, that I could learn to love like that!

Another memorial service was held for the couple in Honduras, where they had served as missionaries for twenty-six years. Cesar Pena, the pastor of the church there, said, "People wanted to follow them—I wanted to follow them—because they followed Jesus with a wholehearted passion."[2]

Pastor Pena went on to describe the twelve churches and more than eighty water wells the Elliotts left behind when they died, a testament to their faithfulness to the Great Commission.

In reality, these missionaries "died" years earlier, when they allowed God's purpose for their lives to supplant their own. This surrender gave them peace in the midst of chaos, a peace evident in an e-mail Jean sent home just days before she was murdered:

> We are happy to be here in Iraq, and our calling has been confirmed. This is a very special time for us, and God is so REAL. No matter what happens, we are in His hands, and we know that we are where we should be.[3]

Like another martyred missionary, Jim Elliot, Larry and Jean willingly "gave up something that they could not keep to gain something that they could not lose," and many others have been encouraged to do the same by their example.

Jeff's group in Mosul experienced supernatural protection, and the Elliotts' group was massacred. But both had this in common: Each was doing the work they had been called to do, and Jesus Christ was glorified as a result. Both groups emerged from their ordeals victorious—one granted additional time to make a difference on this earth, and the other taken home for a victory celebration. Both teams had learned to approach their battles with a *bulletproof mindset*, which made them invincible—in every way that mattered.

In Philippians 1:20, Paul wrote, "I eagerly expect and hope that I will in no way be ashamed, but will have sufficient courage so that now as always Christ will be exalted in my body, whether by life or by death."

What both of these missionary groups did was to eagerly pursue God's purpose in their lives, trusting Him with the results. They were concerned less with their own personal security than they were with their standing before their Commander. They lived well, and in the latter case, they died well.

PARADOX

There is a paradox here that's troubled me at times. In Luke 21:16–19, Jesus seems to contradict Himself on this issue of safety for believers:

> "You will be betrayed even by parents, brothers, relatives and friends, and they will put some of you to death. All men will hate you because of me. But not

a hair of your head will perish. By standing firm you will gain life."

What? How does that add up? How can some of us be put to death, yet realize the promise that "not a hair of your head will perish"?

The answer can only be found in a radically different concept of safety.

Jesus sees things from His Father's perspective. In His eyes, the passage from this world into eternity looks more like a coming-of-age, or a rite of passage. It's a *beginning* of something much more than it is an end of something. Remember your high school graduation? Caps and gowns, hugs, high fives, and perhaps a few tears. It's a bittersweet occasion marking the passing of one phase of life, but the sadness is overshadowed by the anticipation of the many experiences awaiting you on the road ahead.

Paul explains the passage into eternity using similar terms in 2 Corinthians 5:4. The apostle was ready to be done with this life. Why? Because he wanted to be dead? Far from it! Paul wanted to finally experience what it means to be truly alive!

For while we are in this tent, we groan and are burdened, because we do not wish to be unclothed but to be clothed with our heavenly dwelling, *so that what is mortal may be swallowed up by life.* (emphasis mine)

Our Lord's view of safety is vastly different from that of the world. To Him, our earthly dwelling does not represent life, but death. Paul wrote, "Who will rescue me from this body of death?" (Romans 7:24). We see life being swallowed by death, but Christ saw death being swallowed by Life—with a capital *L*! This is how He could say, "Some of you will be put to death…but not a hair on your head will perish."

Jim Elliot, martyred by the Auca Indians in Ecuador in 1956, demonstrated Christ's perspective in a letter to his brother when he wrote, "You are immortal until your work is finished." But Elliot's focus was never on living a long and comfortable life. Instead, his prayer was this:

> God, I pray Thee, light these idle sticks of my life and may I burn up for Thee. Consume my life, my God, for it is Thine. I seek not a long life, but a full one, like You, Lord Jesus.[4]

Jim Elliot's prayers were answered. He lived a full, adventurous life—one which the world would say was cut short when he was brutally murdered attempting to reach a remote tribe with the gospel. But Elliott looked at life differently than the world does. To him, what mattered most was his effectiveness for the kingdom of God. As it turned out, his martyrdom gave rise to a tidal wave of young missionary volunteers. And after Jim's widow went to live with the Aucas—the very ones who murdered her husband—showing them the meaning of forgiveness, the tribe was converted almost in its entirety.

If Jim Elliot had lived and ministered till he was one hundred, he could not have had a greater impact for the kingdom of Christ. This spirit warrior understood that risk has much less to do with the external hazards in life than with his standing in the kingdom of the Most High God.

That's what this book is all about. About risk and why we shun it, but shouldn't always do so. About true safety and security that extend far beyond the brief candle that is this lifetime and reach into the endless years of light and true life in the presence of our Savior. Throughout history, this understanding has enabled men and women to be willing, even joyful, when enduring hardship, uncertainty, pain, and death. From their examples, I can learn to be a more elite soldier for Christ.

And so can you.

Life is not a journey to the grave
with the intention of arriving safely in
a pretty and well preserved body, but rather
to skid in broadside, thoroughly used up,
totally worn out, and loudly proclaiming,
"Wow, what a ride!"

ANONYMOUS

* ★ ★

TWO

WHAT IS "SAFE"?

Y*our children are not safe, anywhere, at any time."*
This postscript was scrawled on a note found taped to a tree in Ashland, Virginia. A tree very near where a man had just been shot in the stomach as he entered a Ponderosa steak house with his wife. He was the twelfth victim of the DC Sniper.

And this time, the madman had left a message: *Your children are targets.*

The community took the message seriously. Just twelve days earlier, a thirteen-year-old boy had been shot while entering his school. In three weeks' time, the unknown gunman had managed to sow fear throughout an entire region—several million people—that bordered on paralysis. People could be seen sprinting to their cars in Wal-Mart parking lots, zigzagging like soldiers advancing across a no-man's-land. Parents kept their children home from school, and those who did attend class were barricaded inside the school building doing "sniper drills."

Recess was canceled. Indefinitely.

A SCENARIO OF FEAR

Business at the Aspen Hill Shell slowed to a barely-profitable trickle. The gas station sat on a busy street corner in Aspen Hill, Maryland, the epicenter of the sniper's attacks. One of the first shootings had taken place at the Mobil station across the street. Black-and-yellow crime-scene tape, flapping wildly in the chilly autumn breeze, still cordoned off the pump where it happened. No one but the reporters wanted to go near it.

Rumors about the identity of the shooter were rampant. News reports advised residents to be on the lookout for a white box van—which narrowed the search to about half a million vehicles in the greater Washington DC area. Some said it was the work of terrorists; others said it was a deranged ex-soldier. No one knew for sure. Everyone was afraid.

Almost everyone.

The Shell station attendant, locked behind bulletproof glass with the cash register, glanced up when an older mini-van pulled up to the pumps. A minute later, he looked up again, puzzled. It wasn't that there weren't any other customers filling up. There were. And minivans in this area were as common as streetlights. What drew his attention was that the man didn't immediately climb back into his vehicle after starting the pump.

The attendant had gotten used to watching customers hurriedly swipe their credit cards and then jump back into their vehicles as soon as the fuel was flowing. The few who paid in cash sometimes actually duckwalked to his window to pay. During the nearly three weeks since the random shootings had begun, the fear and apprehension in the air had become almost palpable.

But this man was different. He was smiling. And relaxed. He chatted with a young boy, presumably his son, who then headed for the windshield squeegee.

Other people were looking, too. With mouths open. Incredulous.

A woman in a BMW pulled up to the pump marked "Full Service" opposite the man and stopped. After a moment, when no attendant arrived to fill her tank, she looked irritated and began honking the horn. Exasperated, she rolled down her window and shouted toward the clerk behind the bulletproof glass, "Come on! I need some gas! Where's the guy?" She had a brash northeastern accent. The man behind the cash register waved his arms and pointed to a piece of paper taped to the pump. It read, "Full service suspended until sniper(s) caught."

She cursed and started to roll up her window. The man who was still waiting for his minivan to fill had witnessed the exchange. He stepped between the pumps and smiled down at the woman in the car.

"Ma'am," he said, "I'll pump your gas for you. Go ahead and pop the cover."

Caught off guard, the woman fairly gaped at him.

"Well, um…sure," she answered after a moment. "But shouldn't you get back in your car? Aren't you worried you'll be the sniper's next victim?"

The man laughed. "Not in the least."

She harrumphed. "What are you, bulletproof or something?"

"Or something."

"Well, at the very least, make that boy get inside where it's safe."

The man looked back at his son, who was merrily slathering window cleaner all over the windows of the van. He smiled slightly. "Oh, he doesn't have anything to be afraid of."

The woman looked at him like he'd just told her he was a poached egg. "That's a bit irresponsible, don't you think? Didn't you see the sniper's warning the other day? He said, 'Your children are not safe'!"

The man looked at her for a moment, forming his words carefully. "The boy's safety has nothing to do with whether or not there's a sniper on the loose."

"Oh? So he's immortal, too?"

"Until God is finished with him here, yes."

"Oh, I see. God is protecting you."

"He has a plan for both of us that ten snipers couldn't ruin."

"Well, why didn't He protect the man who was murdered over there the other day?" She motioned across the street.

"I don't know," he said thoughtfully. "Maybe it's none of my business. God's ways aren't our ways."

She began rummaging in her purse. "I'm not sure I like God's ways."

"I don't always like them, either. But I trust them."

The gas pumped clicked off. The man replaced the nozzle and the BMW's gas cap. The woman mumbled a thank-you and handed him a twenty. She watched as he strode to the window and paid the attendant. His gait exuded confidence, but somehow not bravado.

The man returned with her change and wished her well. "It was nice talking with you," he said, then turned toward his minivan, which his son had nearly squeegeed clean from top to bottom.

"Just one thing," the woman called after him. "What if you're wrong?"

He turned to face her. "What do you mean?"

"What if tomorrow morning *you* become the sniper's next victim?"

"Then I'll be lunching with my Creator at His banquet table. I can think of worse things. I didn't say God would protect me from harm. I said He has a plan for me. I don't have a death wish; it's just that either way, I win."

She smirked. "I wish I could feel that kind of faith."

"Faith is a decision, ma'am, not a feeling."

"Mister Bulletproof, huh? Well, it must be nice."

The window rolled up, and the car edged forward into the morning traffic.

SIEGE MENTALITY

The story above is fictional, but very true to life to those dark and fearful days of October 2002. I lived in the DC area where the sniper killings took place. People sat morbidly affixed to their televisions for days, afraid to venture from their homes. Many Christians—even some in my own church—refused to attend Sunday services; others barricaded themselves inside their homes and nearly worried themselves sick.

One distressed woman posted a plea for help on my website during this time, fear radiating from every word.

SUBJECT: STRESS, NEED HELP!

Can anyone tell me how to deal with the unbelievable amount of stress we are dealing with here in VA, MD, and DC?

They just had a news conference that had a note from the sniper saying, "Your children are not safe anywhere, at any time." Folks, they are now talking about closing all the schools for an indefinite amount of time. I think it's very easy to spout opinions but I'm looking for real help. It's like we are living in a surreal universe where nothing is the same as before. I'm not very religious—but I do believe in a higher power. This morning I heard huge helicopters over my house and thought, *Is this war?*

When does it stop? Why is it happening to us? Weren't anthrax and 9/11 enough? This is real, people. We need help. I need help. It's not a TV show.

Washington DC is a dangerous place, at least as the world defines danger. Before 1996, the city's pro basketball team was named the Washington Bullets. However, the ownership decided that the name was too violent—and maybe a little too close to home. (The joke going around was that they had decided to make the name less violent by simply calling themselves the Bullets.) And so they became the Washington Wizards.

In a normal year, Washington DC experiences, on average, five killings a week, not including those in surrounding counties in Maryland and Virginia. Known as America's murder capital, our nation's seat of power consistently turns in the highest per-capita homicide rate of any major U.S. city.

Most days, people who live and work in the District hardly give these statistics a passing thought. But when John Allen Muhammad and Lee Malvo went on their shooting spree, eventually killing ten and wounding three in the mid-Atlantic region, suddenly *everyone* became aware of the danger. The collective anxiety in the area spiked. People stayed indoors. School programs and sporting events were canceled. Citizens adopted a sort of siege mentality.

What's most interesting about this phenomenon is that, in actuality, people who went about their business as usual were probably *safer*, from a statistical standpoint. Normally, the most dangerous thing you can do in the DC metro area is drive to work. Traffic is so bad that, in some places, just getting to one's destination could qualify as a challenging stunt on NBC's *Fear Factor*. But while the snipers were at large, far fewer people were on the roads, resulting in a much safer commute.

Couple this with the irony that statistically we are more likely to be killed or injured in our own homes, and it becomes clear you'd be safer going about your business than barricading yourself in your house.

A year before this reign of terror, our community suffered through another brush with seemingly random death. Remember the anthrax scare? Anonymous letters containing the chemical agent were mailed to various locations in the country, eventually causing the deaths of five people. Government buildings and mail-handling centers were closed down and invaded by hazmat teams wearing biohazard suits and gas masks. Many citizens refused to take their mail or requested that the postman put it in a box on the porch until the scare had passed. The rumor mill was in high gear as everyone speculated about what would happen next. Another 9/11-style attack?

WHAT ARE YOU AFRAID OF?

So what are *you* afraid of?

Economic downturn?

Dust mites?

Carbon-monoxide poisoning?

SUV rollovers?

An environmental disaster?

Acid-reflux disease?

When people in China's Guangdong Province began dying from a mysterious virus with flu-like symptoms in November 2002, it took Chinese officials nearly four months to announce it to the rest of the world. By then, unsuspecting travelers had transported the virus—now known as Sudden Acute Respiratory Syndrome, or SARS—all over the world.

Governments immediately slammed their borders shut to people visiting from the Far East, but it was too late. Eventually, more than one thousand people died worldwide, and businesses from professional sports teams to Chinese restaurants in New York felt the sting. Trips were canceled, business meetings postponed. Mass hysteria could be created in an airport or subway by someone having a coughing fit after swallowing a piece of gum.

What are you afraid of? Losing your job? Flesh-eating bacteria? Radon? There is quite a smorgasbord of choices.

Maybe you're fearful of dying young. Or perhaps living too long with no retirement savings. How about financial ruin, or cancer? Maybe losing your hair, your health, your figure? Perhaps you're afraid for your children—you're worried something will happen to them or that they will make bad choices.

And don't forget about terrorism. And weapons of mass destruction. And mad cow disease. And drive-by shootings. There could be another plunge in the stock market. You could experience impotence.

We live in a society being eaten alive by anxiety.

Sadly, Christians aren't immune to this pandemic of fear. We find ourselves worrying about all of the forces beyond our control that could do damage to us and our families—everything from tainted water to roving psychopaths. Believers have the added anxiety of watching our religious freedom being eroded. The use of antidepressants has soared to an all-time high, a trend affecting people both inside and outside the church. Fear is all around us.

Shouldn't Christians take a different view, though? What is truly dangerous or risky for the believer? The Bible has plenty to say about how we should handle these things. For instance, in 366 different places, Scripture tells us specifically *not* to be afraid. Think about it. That's one command for every day of the year—including leap years! The only thing we *are* commanded to fear is God Himself. As students of the Bible, should the chaos that we see around the world surprise us? After all, Luke 21:9 reminds us, "These things must happen."

I pitied the woman who wrote me, so distraught over the DC Sniper killings. After mulling her letter over a bit, I sat down and posted a long reply. Here are a few excerpts:

I live here, too. This last killing was only a couple of miles from the church that my family and I attend twice a week. This is certainly getting surreal, but let me tell you something.

I'm not worried or scared in the least. Am I crazy? Perhaps, but let me tell you why. My worldview goes something like this:

A. God is all-powerful and created everything, including me. And He did it for a reason. I'm not just floating through this life; I've got a reason for being here.

B. Over and over again, God's Word tells me that I don't need to be afraid of death. Here is one example: "Do not be afraid of those who kill the body but cannot kill the soul. Rather, be afraid of the One who can destroy both soul and body in hell" (Matthew 10:28).

What does that mean? It means that if you fear God, your whole concept of fear and risk changes. I've heard it said, "To risk all on Christ is to end all risk."

Does that mean that trusting God to do what's best for you makes you less likely to be the sniper's next victim? No, perhaps not from a statistical perspective. What it means is that your personal safety has much less to do with your external circumstances than it does with your standing before God. If you are pursuing the purpose for which you were created, there is no safer place that you can be, even if you are getting shot at. But what if you are pursuing your own objectives, outside of His purpose? Well, you'd better put on a helmet, even if you are sitting on your couch. It's that simple.

Notice that I didn't say "trusting God to protect you from harm." I said "trusting God to do what's best for you." There's a difference. If you have children, you know that sometimes, because you love them, you allow them to go through a difficult circumstance so that they will build character and eventually turn into mature adults. God does the same with us. We don't always understand why He allows tragedies in life, but we can rest assured that He knows where we are and what is happening. And He can help us grow and mature so that we can gain a better understanding of who He is and how much He loves us.

Here are another couple of verses that speak to this issue:

> "Who of you by worrying can add a single hour to his life?" (Matthew 6:27)

> All the days ordained for me were written in your book before one of them came to be. (Psalm 139:16)

So if every day in your life has already been written, GO LIVE IT! Sniper or no sniper!

Some might say that this kind of "If I die, I die" mentality is fatalistic. But I'd disagree. I eagerly look forward to experiencing heaven, but want very much to leave a mark on eternity before I go—and bring as many people as possible to that big, everlasting party with me. For this reason, I cling to every moment of life that I am given. Every day that I wake up tells me God still has more for me to do here. And when I adopt this point of view, my life turns into one great big adventure.

As Christians, our concept of what is risky or dangerous should look much different from that of the world. We have a tremendous opportunity, living in these scared-stiff times, to model to the world the confidence that comes from knowing that God holds us in the palm of His hand, and that nothing happens apart from His will. The Bible tells us that Christ's followers are supposed to know "the peace of God, which transcends all understanding" (Philippians 4:7); and yet many of us today are not at peace.

Yes, the world is, and always has been, a dangerous place to live. And while the title of this book is *Bulletproof*, I don't want to give you the impression that we are invincible—at least, not in a physical sense.

By the time you read the last page, however, I hope you will have an idea of what it means to have a bulletproof mindset. A mindset that enables you to face adversity head-on. A mindset where fear dissolves into faith.

★ ★ ★

THREE

WHOM SHALL I FEAR?

Fear God. Nothing else.

The Bible clearly tells us that only when we develop a healthy fear of Him will we know true peace.

But Satan loves to pervert God's intentions and our emotions, twisting healthy feelings into sinful ones. Love is warped into lust, our appetite for joy is diluted to the pursuit of mere fun, and a healthy fear of God is morphed into anxiety over things that He, in fact, controls.

Just as worshiping creation rather than the Creator takes us into idolatry, *fearing* anything in creation short-circuits our faith. A healthy fear of God, on the other hand, breeds confidence and security—the makings of a strong and attractive faith.

Aristotle defined *confidence* as the opposite of fear. "Confidence," he wrote, "is the hope (anticipation), accompanied by a mental image, of things conducive to safety as being near at hand, while causes of fear seem to be either nonexistent or far away."[5]

Isn't God "near at hand"? Maybe it doesn't feel like it

sometimes, but that is why courage stems from a decision, not a feeling. It's not something you are; it's something you *do*.

We can gain confidence by *cultivating* a healthy fear of God. By working and dwelling on it, reminding ourselves constantly that God will discipline the child who cannot discipline himself.

Yes, *fear* God.

F-E-A-R.

This is more than simply "have respect for Him" or "be in awe of Him." We should do both of those things, but there is more to it than that. When I was a child, I respected my dad and found him either awesome or awful, depending on how obedient I had been. I can recall numerous times when my friends and I contemplated doing something we knew he wouldn't approve of, and I would beg off, saying, "Sorry, guys, my dad would *kill* me."

Obviously, I didn't mean that literally. But what I knew beyond any doubt was that there would be serious consequences if I disobeyed my father. True, this fear of my dad's displeasure was really a self-centered fear—I knew he'd punish me and it would hurt. I now know, however, that it saved me from a whole lot worse. Some of those sins I toyed with in my mind could have led to a miserable, wasted life. So fearing my father in this way was very appropriate. It's the same with God.

WEIGH THE DANGER

This is a God who takes our sin personally. A God so holy that because of one man's sin, an entire world was separated from Him. A God whose wrath killed children because of the sins of their fathers, killed livestock because of the sins of their owner, and turned a woman to salt for simply glancing over her shoulder. He's a God whose fury caused entire civilizations to be wiped from the face of the earth. His is a righteous anger that burned so hot, it could be extinguished only by the blood of the One who was sinless—His own Son.

This is not a mild Santa Claus deity. God is not to be trifled with. With this in mind, doesn't it strike you as dangerous to value your own desires and comfort more than His commands?

Look at this passage from God's own Word:

> If we deliberately keep on sinning after we have received the knowledge of the truth, no sacrifice for sins is left, but only a *fearful expectation of judgment* and of raging fire that will consume the enemies of God. Anyone who rejected the law of Moses died without mercy on the testimony of two or three witnesses. How much more severely do you think a man deserves to be punished who has trampled the Son of God under foot, who has treated as an unholy thing the blood of the covenant that sanctified him, and who has insulted the Spirit of grace? For we know him who said, "It is mine to avenge; I will repay," and again, "The Lord will judge his people." *It is a dreadful thing to fall into the hands of the living God.* (Hebrews 10:26–31, emphasis mine)

Wow.

Think of it this way. Would you rather be charging into enemy lines with the blessing and favor of the Almighty or sitting on your couch without it? Which would be more dangerous, really?

In and of itself, being afraid of something is not sinful. Fear is a feeling, and you can't help feelings. Fear, however, can be both the *effect* of sin and the *cause* of it. Fear can make me take the "easy" way over the right one, or the sin that I commit can allow fear into my life.

Fear is the first recorded negative emotion. The Genesis account reveals that fear entered the world on the heels of original sin, giving rise to the world's first recorded game of hide-and-seek. God came walking in the garden looking for Adam and Eve and found them hiding. (Hiding in the bushes…*from God?*)

God called out to Adam, who answered, "I heard you in the garden, and I was afraid because I was naked; so I hid" (Genesis 3:10).

Up to that point, Adam and Eve had no *reason* to fear anything. Even God. In perfect harmony with His plans, the first couple had no cause to dread His wrath. Perfect obedience equals perfect safety.

But God loved Adam and Eve enough to leave the gate open—to give them the opportunity to walk away from His love if they so chose. Even though He knew the outcome ahead of time, and the ultimate cost their decisions would have on Him personally, He gave them freedom. But not before spelling out clearly what the consequences would be if they chose to rebel. So Adam and Eve, at least on some level, knew what they were getting into.

I'm always puzzled when people refer to Adam and Eve's sin as a "fall from grace." It seems that the first man and woman didn't fall from grace but, rather, *into* it. Before they sinned, there was no need for grace.

We know the rest of the story. Adam and Eve sinned, and God, true to His nature, allowed them to bear the consequences of their choices. They experienced His wrath, and learned what it means to feel holy fear.

But Satan didn't stop with the initial temptation. His objective was to destroy Adam and Eve, and all mankind, so he set about perverting everything good that God had given them. He twisted their rightful fear of God's righteous fury into a fear of death, of pain, and even of life itself. All other forms of fear are perversions or mutations of the fear of God.

From cover to cover, the Bible maps out a formula for exactly why the fear of God is so good for us—and why we never have to fear anyone or anything else. The short version? Get to know God and you will have a good life that will impact your family for generations to come.

When we break this formula down to its component parts, we get a clearer understanding of how this process works. It goes something like this:

Know God → Fear God → Obey God → Make Good Choices → Gain Wisdom → Please God → Be Safe → Live Long and Prosper → Pass On the Knowledge to Your Progeny

KNOW GOD

Dwelling on who God is will help us fear Him in the right way. God is an all-knowing, all-powerful, benevolent King with our best interests in mind and a job for us. He will not be mocked or made a fool of. To call yourself one of His and then reflect poorly on His character is one of the riskiest things you could ever do. Check out Exodus 34:6–7:

> And he passed in front of Moses, proclaiming, "The LORD, the LORD, the compassionate and gracious God, slow to anger, abounding in love and faithfulness, maintaining love to thousands, and forgiving wickedness, rebellion and sin. Yet he does not leave the guilty unpunished; he punishes the children and their children for the sin of the fathers to the third and fourth generation."

FEAR GOD

The book of Genesis tells the story of Joseph, who was sold into slavery by his jealous brothers. God used this apparent tragedy to prepare and position this young man to save his family in a time of great famine. In Genesis 42:18–20, Joseph, now prime minister of the Egyptian empire, sends his humbled brothers back to Israel to retrieve his youngest brother, Benjamin:

> On the third day, Joseph said to them, "Do this and you will live, *for I fear God*: If you are honest men, let one of your brothers stay here in prison, while the rest of you go and take grain back for your starving households. But you must bring your youngest brother to me, so that your words may be verified and that you may not die." This they proceeded to do. (emphasis mine)

Joseph pointed to his fear of God as the anchor in his value system. It was the unshakable guarantee that he would not treat his brothers unfairly.

Leviticus 25:43 gives this instruction to kings, "Do not rule over them ruthlessly, but fear your God." No matter what your station in life, the fear of God is magnetic north on a properly functioning moral compass.

OBEY GOD → MAKE GOOD CHOICES

In Exodus 1:16, Pharaoh ordered two Hebrew midwives to kill any male Hebrew babies that they helped deliver. But in verse 17, we're told that the midwives "feared God and did not do what the king of Egypt had told them to do."

They let the boys live. The women feared God more than they feared Pharaoh. And because this fear anchored their worldview, they obeyed God instead of man and were rewarded for their faithfulness with families of their own.

GAIN WISDOM → PLEASE GOD → BE SAFE

The Bible lists the fear of God as the first step to wisdom (see Proverbs 1:7; Job 28:28; Psalm 111:10). God's wisdom is not like the wisdom of the world, however, which comes from scientific study and rational thought. By the world's standards, God's wisdom often seems irrational—or paradoxical at best. For instance:

"So the last will be first, and the first will be last." (Matthew 20:16)

"For whoever wants to save his life will lose it, but whoever loses his life for me will save it." (Luke 9:24)

Godly wisdom begins with humbling oneself and being obedient. Obedience leads to sound judgment and discernment, which allow us to make good choices that please God.

Solomon wrote:

> My son, preserve sound judgment and discernment, do not let them out of your sight; they will be life for you, an ornament to grace your neck. Then you will go on your way in safety, and your foot will not stumble...when you lie down, your sleep will be sweet. Have no fear of sudden disaster or of the ruin that overtakes the wicked, for the LORD will be your confidence and will keep your foot from being snared. (Proverbs 3:21–26)

LIVE LONG AND PROSPER → PASS ON THE KNOWLEDGE TO YOUR PROGENY

In Deuteronomy 5:32–33, God tells Moses:

> So be careful to do what the LORD your God has commanded you; do not turn aside to the right or to the left. Walk in all the way that the LORD your God has commanded you, so that you may live and prosper and prolong your days in the land that you will possess.

God didn't want the Israelites to fear Him out of some self-absorbed tyrannical power trip. He intended their fear to lead to obedience, so that "it might go well with them and their children forever," so that they might live long and prolong their days.

Why would God want us to have long lives here on a fallen planet? Won't heaven be much better? Why would He want to keep us here? Paul has an answer for us:

In a large house there are articles not only of gold and silver, but also of wood and clay; some are for noble purposes and some for ignoble. If a man cleanses himself from the latter, *he will be an instrument for noble purposes*, made holy, useful to the Master and prepared to do any good work. (2 Timothy 2:20–21, emphasis mine)

Special operations soldiers are held to a higher standard than the rest of the Army. They are the cream of the crop, men who have been willing to pay a higher price in training in order to be given a special part in the real mission. They are elite, set apart from the other soldiers, willing to do anything, anywhere, anytime.

Then there are soldiers who are in it simply for the college money. They do as little as possible in order to receive their benefits. These are the ones who end up guarding a concrete block in some forsaken outpost, while other soldiers do the fighting.

God wants to give us important, meaningful work to do here on earth. But we have to decide how much we are willing to participate. He will accomplish His plan with or without us, but He *wants* to include us. The bottom line is that a long life doesn't have much appeal if it has no purpose. Meaningless existence is the very definition of hell.

God, however, offers us a long life filled with significance in pursuit of His purpose. Fearing Him will put us in the right frame of mind to allow His will to be accomplished in and through us. God wants us to live long here on earth so that we will have the maximum opportunity to experience the joy of being in His service.

THE SAFEST PLACE TO BE

Safety, however, does not mean comfort. It doesn't even equate to lack of danger, as the world understands it. Obeying God, however, is *always* the safest course of action, even if He orders you to your death. There's a paradox for you!

These truths only seem paradoxical, however, because we use one word (*safe*) to express two ideas. So what is safe?

The world defines safe as "secure from danger, harm, injury, or evil." The Bible's definition is much simpler: being on God's side. When we step outside of His will, we actually position ourselves between the Commander and victory. Now *that* is a dangerous place to be! Think of it this way: Would you rather accomplish all of your earthly goals without God's blessing or fail at your objectives in order to help accomplish His and receive His blessing?

Look at these words from the book of Job, paying attention to the fact that it says the "darkness will become *like* morning," meaning that the darkness will still be there, but your perspective will change.

> "Yet if you *devote your heart to him*
> and stretch out your hands to him,
> if you *put away the sin* that is in your hand

and allow no evil to dwell in your tent,
then you will lift up your face without shame;
you will *stand firm and without fear.*
You will surely forget your trouble,
recalling it only as waters gone by.
Life will be brighter than noonday,
and darkness will become like morning.
You will be secure, because there is hope;
you will look about you and take your rest in safety.
You will lie down, with *no one to make you afraid,*
and many will court your favor."
(Job 11:13–19, emphasis mine)

Consider the biblical formula again:

1. To know God is to fear Him.
2. To fear Him is to obey.
3. Obedience brings good choices.
4. Good choices make you wiser.
5. Wisdom (which is *exercised* knowledge) pleases God and keeps you safe from His wrath.
6. That safety will give you a long and fruitful life.
7. Your children and grandchildren will share in this legacy of faith.

What's not to like about that? When we come to understand God's nature through the study of His Word, it will help us to fear Him in the right way. Armed with this fear, we have absolutely nothing else to be afraid of.

* * *

FOUR

RETHINKING RISK

G etu Mulleta lives in Ethiopia with his wife and five children. Miles from electricity or running water, the Mulleta's 326-square-foot home is a three-room hovel constructed of dung—yes, dung—mixed with straw. Over 90 percent of the population in this rural area has no access to clean water.

Though Getu and his wife, Zenebu, both work an average of a hundred hours a week, their annual household income is less than $400. Their children don't attend school because they can't afford books and clothing.

Several years ago, the publishers of the book *Material World* sent a photographer to live with the Mulletas for one week. His assignment was the same as that of sixteen other photojournalists staying with families in thirty other countries, from Bhutan and Brazil to Iceland and Vietnam: to capture on film daily life among the host families, each chosen because they typified the average household in their respective countries. The families were also asked to talk about their lives, their values, and their aspirations for the future.

While life is often difficult and frustrating for the Mulleta family in Ethiopia, they find solace in their strong belief in Jesus Christ. When photographer Shawn Henry asked them what they would like to have in the future, it is notable that chief among their wishes was peace in their area and around the world. Getu explained that "only peace everywhere would enable everyone everywhere to share in life's bounty."[6]

That same year, another photographer spent a week with the Abdulla family in Kuwait. They also have five children, but their circumstances contrast dramatically with those of the Mulletas. At just under five thousand square feet, their home has four bathrooms, servants' quarters, a bar, and an indoor swimming pool. No dung in sight, I daresay. The family owns five telephones, four automobiles, two televisions, and a computer. The parents and older children are college educated, and the family spends its days watching MTV via satellite, shopping at the mall, and chatting with friends on their cellular phones.

Mr. Abdulla quips that in Kuwait, when the going gets tough, the tough go shopping. What are their wishes for the future? Among other things, a fishing boat—and more income.

Which family does yours most resemble?

WHAT DO I REALLY "DESERVE"?

Most American families would identify much more closely with the Kuwaiti family. We live in a culture obsessed with comfort and safety, and we allow ourselves to believe that if we just had a bit more money (and maybe a boat) things would be better. Somehow, we've come to believe that we *deserve* to be insulated from every form of insecurity. Just look at the messages thrown at us from the advertisements we see every day.

From an ad for a hotel chain: "Our guest suites are the ideal choice for that superbly comfortable and pleasurable vacation *you so richly deserve.*"

Or consider this slogan for earmuffs: "The comfort you need, the quality *you deserve.*"

An on-line beauty page for women declares, "Most of us tend to put pleasing others before ourselves, which can be both tiring and emotionally draining. So take some time off to pamper yourself, because *you deserve it!*"

You deserve comfort. You deserve happiness. You deserve a break. You deserve the finest. You deserve freedom from fear. You deserve security. You deserve quality earmuffs.

It's the mantra of Western society, directed at us constantly, in countless ways, both explicit and implicit. The media tells me that I should pursue comfort and security by running from stress and insulating myself from risk to the greatest extent possible.

Why? *Because I deserve it.*

I'm not likely to look very skeptically at these claims, because deep down I *want* to believe them! I'm wired to be self-centered. Unfortunately, this attitude *magnifies* fear in my life—it gives me one more thing to worry about. I mean, *am* I getting what I deserve? Why aren't I? And who's responsible if I'm not? Can I sue?

The community where I live is populated by some of the most affluent people on earth, many of whom—though insured to the hilt—are more fearful, stressed-out, and unhappy than ever. As it turns out, a life that revolves around *me* is meaningless. Chasing after fun has proven to be folly.

When my wife and I first bought our farm, it didn't take long for me to realize that it would take a tremendous amount of *stuff* to keep the farm running. I needed chainsaws, a wood splitter, a tractor, a mower, a couple of four-wheelers, a farm truck. I was making good money at the time, and so as the months went by after we moved in, our front yard began to accumulate more and more *stuff*.

One day I came home with a bulldozer. "But honey," I said by way of explanation, "we need it!" Besides, every man secretly wants to own a tracked vehicle. But I didn't tell her that.

Anyway, that next fall, we had a long spell of rain. It poured for days on end, and I noticed that I was having trouble sleeping. Something was really bothering me. Finally it dawned on me: All of my *stuff* was getting rusty out in the driveway! So I decided to build a garage. But when I sat down and figured out how many stalls I'd need to house my stuff, the total came to eleven. An *eleven*-car garage?

Then it hit me. The more *stuff* I accumulated, the more anxious I became. I didn't own all that stuff. It owned me. The things that were supposed to make my life easier were actually making it worse. So I got rid of virtually everything. The truck, the wood splitter, and yes, the bulldozer. And the anxiety went away. How about that?

Randy Alcorn writes, "The more things we own—the greater their total mass—the more they grip us, setting us in orbit around them."[7]

ON THE SIDELINES?

Instinctively, we know that joy often emerges from great struggle and triumph. Most popular spectator sports include lots of highly-padded and heavily-insured adversity. As spectators, we experience by proxy the challenge, hardship, and accomplishment that takes place on the field. The sweat. The blood. The tension. The tears. It's all there. I know guys who never miss a game of their favorite team and who (one could believe) truly dislike anyone who roots for the competition.

But what purpose does it serve?

At the end of the game, after the expenditure of all that time and emotional energy, no lives have been changed, no lasting difference has been made whatsoever. The world is the same.

Are sports bad? Perhaps it's better put this way: In time of war, *anything* that diverts our efforts from the battle at hand is counterproductive.

Does that mean that we shouldn't watch Monday Night Football? Perhaps it does! We should inspect our actions daily and ask of them, "Is this pastime the most strategic way to use the few brief moments I'm given on earth? Or is it a momentary diversion to ease the boredom of a comfort-seeking life being lived out on the sidelines?"

Lives wasted in the pursuit of comfort do nothing but leave a person's spirit hungry, atrophied from lack of real nourishment and healthy exercise. It's like eating salted peanuts to quench your thirst. Or grabbing a plastic banana for a snack. It may have looked mouthwatering from a distance, but no matter how many fake bananas you accumulate, they will never satisfy your hunger.

REAL RISK, REAL JOY

Fortunately, in comparison, life lived according to God's plan is an overflowing, all-you-can-eat buffet. There is real joy to be had in risking our lives in the pursuit of God's purpose. We are called to live free from anxiety and worry, not by ridding ourselves of all the stress and risk that might come our way, but by trusting God to be our anchor in the midst of crisis.

When I was young, I used to hear the phrase "the peace that passes all understanding" used around our church. This always made me think of another Scripture passage, from Psalm 23: "He makes me lie down in green pastures, he leads me beside quiet waters" (v. 2). I would imagine myself reclining under a tree, looking up at puffy white clouds, listening to the gurgling brook, and hearing songbirds in the branches. Ah, perfect peace.

A very different image now comes to mind when I read this verse.

Instead of soft green grass, whispering breezes, yellow finches, and cotton-ball clouds, I now think of one night in Panama, in combat. I think of Command Sergeant Major Leon-Guerrero, regimental sergeant major of the 75th Ranger Regiment. It was the early morning hours of December 20, 1989. We had just parachuted into Panama during Operation Just Cause, and we found ourselves in the middle of a firefight.

Widely respected and known for his intense personal discipline and incredible physical fitness, CSM Leon-Guerrero pushed himself—and everyone under his command—to their very limits and just a little bit beyond. If this sergeant major was leading your PT run, you knew you were in for a smoker.

At the launch of the Panama invasion, with bullets flying all around in the wee hours of the morning, we looked up from our position to see the sergeant major standing in the middle of a road. He saw us cowering in a ditch beside the road and scowled. Seemingly oblivious to the danger, he stood there and shouted, "Move out, men! We've got a job to do!"

We moved out.

We got up out of that ditch and headed for our objective, both motivated and impressed by this man's example of fearlessness in the heat of battle.

We've got a job to do.

There was something about being reminded that we were there for a purpose that enabled us to drive on in spite of our emotions. And that sense of focused purpose was more powerful than the fear.

The sergeant major's performance that dark morning taught me something I'll never forget. Fear may be contagious, but so is confidence. And confidence can be *constructed* through tough training and self-discipline.

Peace is not the absence of tribulation. God offers to *be our peace* in the midst of hardship.

RUNNING FROM RISK

The more sophisticated and technologically advanced we become as a culture, the more preoccupied we have become with eliminating risk. Any risk. All risk. And the more we identify and quantify those risks, the more money we throw at them! We develop new drugs, pass new protective laws, buy more insurance, add more warning labels,

For example, new security measures added by the airlines since the events of September 11, 2001, have cost taxpayers over $20 billion, not to mention the billions in security surcharges collected on airline tickets. That amounts to nearly $200 per household in the U.S. The increased cost of flying, coupled with increased anxiety about flying after the attacks, mean that more people are choosing to drive when traveling.

Social psychologist David G. Myers writes:

Indeed, the terrorists may still be killing us, in ways unnoticed. If we now fly 20 percent less and instead drive half those unflown miles, we will spend 2 percent more time in motor vehicles. This translates into 800 more people dying as passengers and pedestrians. So in just the next year the terrorists may indirectly kill three times more people on our highways than died on those four fated planes [on September 11].[8]

My friend Tim Miller used to work for the Department of Homeland Security. He had the privilege of sitting in on daily classified threat briefings and knew all about what our government was doing to safeguard the country. When I asked him one day if we are safer now than we were before September 11, he answered, "We are much safer today, because we're more aware."

But despite the measures that have been enacted since that horrible day in 2001, most Americans feel *less* safe than they did before the attacks. There is little doubt that, prior to 9/11, many of us weren't aware of the chances of having heinous acts committed against our country, and so our ignorance allowed us to feel secure. Now that we know better, we feel less secure, even though the chances of anyone hijacking an airplane and flying it into a building again are virtually nil, especially since anyone who tried it would be immediately set upon by all the other passengers and beaten to a pulp. All these safety measures have failed to provide the feeling of security that our nation so desperately seeks.

Perhaps it's because we are searching in the wrong place.

Statistics tell us that we are actually safer in an airplane than we are on our living room couch, so it is apparent that the problem lies in our *perception* of what is dangerous, not in the reality of it. Which is my point exactly.

When I recently proposed putting together a trip to Jordan for people in the Washington DC area, I was immediately turned down. "There's no way that we are going to assume that kind of risk," I was told. Instead, the same group sponsored a trip to New York City, which is statistically *far* more dangerous. Again, it came down to perceived, not actual, risk.

As Christians, our perception of what is dangerous *should be* vastly different from that of the rest of the world, because we hold to a worldview that says everything happens for a reason, according to the will of a sovereign God.

Instead, for many of us, life is a bit less enjoyable than it once was. Remember when spending a day at the beach wasn't tainted by the fear of skin cancer? Or when you could relish a good steak or a sticky bun without worrying about cholesterol or carbohydrates? Or when you could relax on your front porch swing without worrying about contracting the West Nile virus? It can be that way again!

A JOB TO DO

The apostle Paul didn't worry about these kinds of things. He had a job to do and spent his time and effort striving to accomplish his mission. Cholesterol and carbs and the high cost of health insurance didn't seem to bother him much. Neither did assassins, the forces of nature, the Roman government, or venomous snakes. Paul knew where his safety came from. He had an uncanny ability to see things from God's point of view, and so fear wasn't an issue he struggled with very often.

True, there was that episode in Macedonia, when the pressures of ministry had become overwhelming and fears closed in: "This body of ours had no rest, but we were harassed at every turn—conflicts on the outside, fears within." Seeking and finding God's comfort, however, it wasn't long before Paul's joy was "greater than ever" (2 Corinthians 7:5–7).

Paul didn't close his eyes to the dangers around him. But he understood that he had a mission to accomplish, and he never expected it to be a stroll through the rose garden. Whatever was happening around him, Paul pressed on toward the goal and trusted God with the outcome.

When we concern ourselves with pursuing God's purposes, we will almost inevitably find ourselves less comfortable and taking more risks than we would otherwise. But we will also find ourselves more joyful, more fulfilled, and yes, safer in every way that matters. This kind of purpose-driven lifestyle promises to be difficult, but worth it. No one will ever regret following God's leading to join the battle.

The sixteenth-century Heidelberg catechism asks the

question, "What is thy only comfort in life and in death?" The answer gives an important look at the mindset of Christians in centuries past: "That I with body and soul, both in life and death, am not my own, but belong to my faithful Saviour Jesus Christ."[9]

FEAR SELLS

Admittedly, many of the dangers that we are warned of by the media turn out to be overhyped paranoia, designed to boost ratings or to push a product.

I recently did an Internet search on the phrase "may be killing you." You'd be amazed at the number of the things that you could possibly die from (or maybe you wouldn't be). As it turns out, life is deadly! Here's a partial list of what may be killing you at this very moment:

Vitamins
Filtered water
What you eat
Talc
Snoring
Job stress
Electronic waves
Your computer
What you don't know
What your doctor doesn't know

And there's more! Known killers also include your corns, your marriage, bread, your health and beauty products, your pet, nondairy creamer, your house, your office, and the chair you're sitting in while reading this book.

You may also want to consider eliminating these deadly items from your life: meat, carbs, milk, fat and fat substitutes, butter and butter substitutes, salt and salt substitutes, sugar and sugar substitutes, your neighbor's woodstove, second-hand smoke, your cellular phone, popcorn, fruits, and vegetables.

Obviously, many of these "dangers" are exaggerated in order to sell us something. In fact, advertisers find fear to be one of the most effective selling tools. Americans waste billions of dollars each year trying to insure away every form of discomfort. As Tony Campolo says, "Most of us are tiptoeing through life in order to arrive at death as safely as possible."[10]

Sociologist Barry Glassner writes, "A group that raises money for research into a particular disease is not likely to negate concerns about that disease. A company that sells alarm systems is not about to call attention to the fact that crime is down.... We all pay one of the costs of [fear]: huge sums of money go to waste."[11]

NO - RISK INSURANCE

The truth is, without a strong anchor of faith, the world can be a very scary place indeed. We don't know what the future holds, so every day brings an element of risk with it. If only we knew the outcome of every one of our actions ahead of time....

But God *does* know what we will face tomorrow.

And through Him—through this God who sees the future in the same moment that He sees our present—we must learn to redefine what it is to be safe and secure. Safe, as the world defines it, means security from danger, harm, or evil. The Christian perspective should be decidedly different—more like "proximity to God's purpose, regardless of danger, harm, or evil."

Nothing is risky for Him.

Seen any SUV commercials lately? Clearly, Americans pride themselves on their rugged individualism, toughness, and preparedness. But no matter how rugged we think we may be, we simply cannot be equipped for everything. Every day, a thousand different things *could* happen that we cannot possibly imagine, much less prepare for. But that doesn't stop us from spending our time, energies, and resources in a futile attempt to reduce our risk of calamity to zero.

It's impossible. It isn't even logical.

There is a certain subculture among Christians that believes strongly in being prepared for any emergency that may arise. These were most active in the months leading up to the year 2000. Remember Y2K? People bought up power generators like they were facing a new ice age, while stockpiling food and supplies for the great meltdown.

But it never came.

There's certainly nothing wrong with preparing for the worst. I'm just asserting that the most important preparation we can make is *spiritual*. Why? Because unlike the Y2K bug, spiritual warfare *will* happen. It *is* happening. And it will happen to you. As Paul admonished Timothy, "Physical training is of some value, but godliness has value for all things, holding promise for both the present life and the life to come" (1 Timothy 4:8).

BLACK HAWK DOWN
MOGADISHU, SOMALIA, 1993

During the raid made famous in *Black Hawk Down*, the best-selling book that later became a movie, my friend Jeff Strueker reached a point where he hit a wall physically—and discovered the true value of being spiritually prepared.

Jeff's convoy was dispatched to rescue a wounded Ranger who had fallen from a helicopter. On the way back to base, Jeff's convoy was attacked and one of his men was killed instantly. Arriving back at base with a badly shot-up Humvee, Strueker was informed that a helicopter had been shot down and that they were being sent back out to help evacuate the downed pilots.

At this point, Jeff knew he was about to die.

After what they had just come through, it seemed unlikely they would be able to survive another foray into the city. As he cleaned the blood of his fallen comrade out of the back of his Humvee, Jeff thought, *Tomorrow this will be my blood.* He had just received a letter from his wife, Dawn, informing him that she was pregnant with their first child. *My baby will never know its father.* Jeff was racked with fear and a sense of his own impending doom.

Jeff, however, had a strong faith in God—a faith that became an anchor in the storm. He began praying the prayer he'd read just the day before during his quiet time. It was the same prayer that Jesus prayed in his darkest hour: "Father, if you are willing, take this cup from me." But then Jeff remembered the rest of the prayer: "Yet not my will, but yours be done" (Luke 22:42).

Looking back, Jeff will tell you that was the defining

moment. Everything he'd said he believed came back to stare him in the face. And the last part of that prayer, the part where he surrendered his will to God, was when Jeff won the battle. He still believed he would die that day. But he had the assurance from God that in his death Christ would be glorified, and Jeff's family would remain in God's capable and loving hands either way. And once he surrendered, the fear left and Jeff found peace.

He climbed in his Humvee and drove back into battle.

For the next fourteen hours, the Rangers in Mogadishu endured one of the worst firefights since the Vietnam War, fending off literally thousands of enraged Somalis, but refusing to leave the bodies of their fallen comrades. Eighteen Americans died that night, but Jeff wasn't one of them.

The next day, something strange began to happen. Strueker's buddies were coming to him with questions. "My buddy was killed. Where is he now?" "What if that is me tomorrow?" Rock-hard Rangers who thought they had been prepared for combat were coming to him with tears in their eyes, realizing they had neglected the most important element in training for war—their spiritual fitness. They came to Jeff because they knew he had faith, and they needed to draw on it because they had none of their own.

At that point, Jeff heard a new calling. He wanted nothing more than to help the men that he'd fought beside, and those who would come after them, to be prepared spiritually the next time they faced combat.

Jeff left the Army and went to seminary. Upon graduation, he rejoined the military as a chaplain. Today, as the chaplain for the 2nd Ranger Battalion at Fort Lewis, Washington, Jeff has had the privilege of serving soldiers in combat in Afghanistan and Iraq.

"I don't care how tough you think you are," he likes to tell his fellow Rangers, "there's a situation out there in combat that will bring you to your knees. And when you reach that point, you're going to need what I have."

★ ★ ★

FIVE

IN THE MOMENT OF CRISIS

15 September 1999

Pop! Pop! Pop!

Mike looked up from his desk. *Those sounded like gunshots.*

It was a Wednesday night, and Mike, an associate pastor at Wedgwood Baptist Church in Fort Worth, Texas, was hunkered over a malfunctioning desktop computer when he heard the noise.

He knew the sound from his days as a fire investigator before attending seminary, but it was so strange, so foreign in a church, that he couldn't decide if he'd heard right.

The only thing special about this night's activities was that the usual Wednesday night service had been replaced by a youth rally and concert celebrating the annual "See You at the Pole" event. The band 40 Days was on stage, and several hundred teens were enjoying their set.

Mike got up and went to investigate, hurrying the dozen or so steps through the church's administrative office complex. He reached the door to the foyer and opened it.

People outside were shouting. A man was striding toward him, smoking a cigarette.

Now that's strange, Mike thought. Then he saw what was in the man's other hand.

A semiautomatic pistol.

The man looked up and their eyes met for an instant. The man then coolly raised his arm and pointed the gun at him. Before Mike could react, the man squeezed off two quick shots. Mike didn't stick around to see what would happen next. Instantly in crisis mode, he sprinted down the hallway in the opposite direction. His first thought was of the many kids who were, at that moment, playing in the children's wing of the church.

As he ran, he knew he should make a call for help. The church library had a phone. Mike ducked in and snatched it up, some part of his consciousness noticing the two frantic women already taking refuge there as he dialed 911. He told the dispatcher that he thought there was a shooting in progress at the church. Considering that the gunman had just shot at him, it might seem funny that he wasn't sure. But it just seemed so out of place—so *wrong*—that he couldn't bring himself to believe it.

Dropping the phone onto its cradle, Mike dashed out and continued toward the children's wing. Rounding the corner, he encountered a church custodian draped over a bench, bleeding from a gunshot wound, with several people attending to him. Now he had to accept that this was real. He went back and called 911 again. But it wasn't necessary. By then, distress calls were flooding the emergency dispatch from every available cell phone in the building.

No one will ever know exactly what made Larry Ashbrook drive past several other churches, push his way through the doors of Wedgwood Baptist on that fateful September night, and start killing people. He had never been a member there and was not affiliated with the church in any way. When he entered the building, the custodian approached him and asked that he put out his cigarette. Ashbrook drew a pistol and shot the custodian twice. He then opened fire on several others in the foyer, killing one woman instantly and wounding another.

On his way to the sanctuary he encountered and shot the staff counselor, Kevin Galey, twice in the stomach. Proceeding along the hallway, the gunman saw Mike peering out of the office doorway. After a quick two-shot volley in his direction, Ashbrook turned to enter the sanctuary and began firing at random, moving back and forth among the teens who were still worshiping to the music of 40 Days.

For a few moments, many believed Ashbrook and his pistol were part of some kind of bizarre skit. But when the wounded began screaming and rivulets of blood began to run down the sloped floor under the pews, mass chaos erupted.

Ashbrook fired more than one hundred bullets from two pistols and exploded a pipe bomb that sent shrapnel into the balcony and through the ceiling.

Dr. Ray Pritchard describes what happened next:

Through the screams, shouts, smoke, and bloodshed, a nineteen-year-old young man stood to his feet.

Jeremiah Nietz decided he had seen enough. He wasn't going to stand by and watch his friends be murdered one by one. Facing the gunman, he said, "Sir, you don't need to do that." Ashbrook replied with a foul comment. "I know what you need," said Jeremiah Nietz. "You need Jesus Christ in your life." At that moment the shooter pointed his gun directly at the young man standing only a few feet away. "Shoot me if you want to. I know where I'm going when I die. What about you?" Something in those words seemed to pierce the twisted, evil heart of Larry Gene Ashbrook. He slowly sat down, uttered another swear word, then put the gun to his head and pulled the trigger.[12]

The entire episode lasted about fifteen minutes. It would never be known what drove Ashbrook to this, but whatever it was, many would agree that the reasons had to be more spiritual than physical, mental, or emotional.

And Mike found himself at ground zero.

Time slipped into a blur. Emergency personnel evacuated the church grounds and cordoned off the area. Anxious clusters of church members, family, and friends gathered at the elementary school across the street, everyone frantically searching for information about casualties. Hundreds of media trucks, emergency vehicles, and police cars, all with lights flashing, clogged the streets for blocks in every direction.

Slowly, painfully, the details emerged. Eight were dead, including the gunman. Another seven were wounded, some severely. Mike overheard two members relate that they had seen one of the youth workers who had been shot. They were sure he was dead. Across the room, the man's wife was nearly hysterical, asking if anyone had seen her husband. The two who knew he was dead couldn't bring themselves to break the news to her. But she had to be told. Mike guided her into an adjacent office along with two of her best friends and, as gently as possible, told her the truth. It wasn't easy, but it was the right thing to do.

Anyone who was there that night, and in the weeks following the shootings, will say that Mike, the associate pastor with the knack for organization, was among those who were instrumental in helping the traumatized church get back to its feet and move beyond the tragedy.

Mike went the first four days with almost no sleep, working nonstop to coordinate the hundreds of necessary details, such as overseeing the removal and replacement of blood-stained carpeting and bullet-torn pews and coordinating the offers of support and assistance that flooded in from individuals, businesses, and sister churches. Mike ministered to grieving church members by simply being there, doing his best to be strong and stay faithful to his Protector.

That first week after the shooting, an army of television cameras and news crews prowled the grounds, looking for interviews. Mike stopped answering his phone. Mourners and well-wishers begged for details and tours of the scene. A huge memorial service at Texas Christian University's football stadium was broadcast around the world.

Through it all, Mike worked in the background to hold the church together until the winds of the storm subsided. He'd learned crisis management during his years in the fire department, and those skills had never been more in demand. With a God-given gift for prioritizing challenges at hand and motivating people to get the job done, Mike's skill set precisely matched the overwhelming need of the moment.

It would later be said that the real miracle of that fateful evening was that although the gunman fired over one hundred rounds during the shooting spree, fewer than twenty people had been hit. Ashbrook took his own tortured life with more than a hundred unspent rounds remaining in his weapons.

One other thing. Mike is a big man who fills any doorway, yet days passed before it occurred to him that two of those bullets had struck within inches of him but neither found its mark.

As the days wore on it became clear that God had protected Mike "for such a time as this." God's plan included having him in place to assist in picking up the pieces of the tragedy. God could have used someone else to do it, but He didn't. So for that horrible night, at least, Mike was untouchable. Bulletproof.

WHERE WAS GOD'S PROTECTION?

But what about the seven who were brutally murdered? It appears that they encountered a great evil—and lost. All were committed believers, some of them young teens cut down just as they were beginning their spiritual journeys. Didn't God's protection apply to them? Maybe it would be better to ask if God's *plan* still applied to them.

Kim Jones was at Wedgwood Baptist Church that night.

A recent graduate of TCU, she was actively seeking God's plan for what she should do next. Her heart's desire was to share the good news of Jesus Christ with everyone with whom she came in contact. Kim had spent a previous summer doing mission work in Europe. Upon returning home, she had an opportunity to speak to a group of teens at a youth rally, and her parents captured it on videotape.

In her talk, she told of her extended summer mission experience, frequently moving from one place to another and never being able to unpack her bags. It had been fun, but nothing compared to the joy she felt upon arriving home and being able to sleep in her own bed after a long time abroad.

She told the teens that life here on earth is a lot like her summer European adventure. "We're just backpackers here," she said, smiling. "But when we get to our true home, it will be like taking off our heavy packs and settling into our own comfortable beds."

A short time later, Kim Jones did just that. She was one of those killed in the Wedgwood Church shootings.

Kim's life on earth ended that night—way before anyone could have imagined. Was that also a part of God's plan? After all, she had felt His calling upon her life and wanted more than anything else to share Christ with others. Could any good come from such a nightmare turn of events?

That question may never get answered in this life. But one thing is certain: God used the tragedy to leverage the power of His church around the world. We refer to Kim and those who died as "victims," but the Bible tells us they are *victors* (see Philippians 1:21; 1 Corinthians 15:54).

One of the more than twenty thousand e-mails received

by Wedgwood Baptist Church in the days after the shootings came from a Christian woman in a Middle Eastern country closed to all missionary activity. Non-Muslims who share their religious beliefs with others in that nation face severe consequences. The woman related that for the past twenty years she had been praying that the message of Christianity would someday, somehow, be disseminated in her country. And that very day she had witnessed the memorial service from TCU stadium—and a clear gospel presentation—broadcast on state-sponsored television across her entire nation!

Aired around the globe, the message of hope at that service was witnessed by untold millions. Since the shooting, Wedgwood Baptist Church has been able to minister to many hurting people. Why do they come? Because they know they will find people who can empathize with their suffering.

GOD NEVER WASTES ANYTHING

Stan Jones, Kim's father, lived with his wife in Saudi Arabia, where he worked for an American oil company. Immediately upon hearing news of their daughter's murder, they flew back to Texas.

Mike had been introduced to Kim's parents some months earlier when they were in Fort Worth visiting her at Texas Christian. At that meeting, Mike had assured Stan and his wife, Stephanie, that he would look after Kim and "keep her straight." With a wink, he promised to administer discipline, if needed.

When Stan walked through the church doors the Sunday

after Kim died, he ran into Mike right away. They grabbed each other in an emotional bear hug. Somewhere inside Mike, a dam broke and the tears flowed. Stan and Mike held each other and sobbed.

Both men were gripped by heart-wrenching feelings of utter helplessness and frustrated anger at not having been able to stop the tragic events that led to Kim's death. Yet deep down, they knew there was nothing they could have done. And both readily acknowledged that Kim was now truly home.

For Mike, it wasn't the first time he'd felt this helplessness. In fact, God had begun preparing him for this moment twenty-five years earlier. His wife, Kathy, had been suddenly stricken with botulism and spent weeks in intensive care, hovering near death. They had been married only five years and had two small children. As Mike sat by the bedside of his ailing young wife, he had to face the prospect of life without her, and the fear nearly paralyzed him.

But God had spoken to him through that challenge and made Mike understand that Kathy was His child first and Mike's wife second. Letting God be sovereign over Kathy's life was one of the hardest lessons Mike had ever had to learn. If God wanted Kathy's life, it was His to take, and no matter what, He would be faithful to Kathy, Mike, and the kids.

Giving his own life to Christ hadn't been nearly as difficult as surrendering Kathy to God's plans. It made Mike understand that he was *always* powerless to protect his family. Every day there were an untold number of tragedies that could befall them. The fact is, life would not allow him to choose which crises they would face. But Mike did have a choice: He could choose where to run for refuge when crisis came.

That lesson came in handy on September 15, 1999, when he desperately needed the assurance that God was still in control. Kathy eventually recovered and she says today, "I've learned that God never wastes anything."

Personally, I'm thankful that God didn't take Kathy at that time. I'm also grateful that Mike wasn't left alone to raise those two small children.

Because I was one of them.

★ ★ ★

SIX

NO SAFER PLACE

Unless the LORD watches over the city, the
watchmen stand guard in vain.

PSALM 127:1

A couple of years ago we bought our kids a go-cart. It was just a little one, but the kids had great fun zipping around the loop in our driveway. I did everything I could to ensure their safety, checking to see that no traffic was coming down the drive, making them wear helmets, and specifically forbidding them to drive the go-cart anywhere near the parked vehicles.

I'll admit, I had one very big concern. My biggest fear was that one of the kids would accidentally drive the go-cart underneath our big farm truck, which sat just high enough to clear the go-cart's steering wheel and catch the rider in the throat. This would almost certainly result in a broken neck, or worse.

I tried scare tactics, giving the kids a graphic demonstration.

Pushing the go-cart under the farm truck, I showed them how the bumper would catch a rider at the neck—drawing an ominous line across my throat—if they got careless.

Wide-eyed, my kids listened. They really did. And they were careful to obey and follow my instructions.

But it happened anyway.

One day Kiernan, my seven-year-old daughter, was riding around in the grass inside the parking loop. She was taking it easy and having fun while the other kids and I stood watching her. Not wanting to be in the way, we moved well away from where she was driving, over by the parked vehicles.

Then Kiernan decided she needed to ask me a question. Making a sharp turn in the go-cart, she shot across the gravel over to where we were standing. But instead of applying the brake, Kiernan stomped on the gas, and the little cart barreled right at me! Instinctively, I leaped out of the way—a split second before remembering that the farm truck was right behind me.

I had just enough time to scream, "No, God!" before the impact. Kiernan careened into the farm truck, hitting it so hard that it knocked her sandals off. Horrified, I ran to her. I just knew she had broken her neck. Heart in my throat, I pulled the go-cart away from the truck and checked her out.

My little girl was badly shaken but miraculously uninjured! How could this be? Closer examination revealed that because the truck was parked on an uneven spot on the driveway, the bumper was sitting half an inch lower than normal—just enough to catch the steering wheel of the go-cart and stop it from going completely under the truck.

Half an inch.

I felt like I should yell at Kiernan. Give her a lecture. Instead, I hugged her tightly and wept.

For some time after that mishap, I kept raking myself over the coals. The scene played itself over and over in my mind, leaving me disgusted that I had jumped out of the way of the speeding go-cart. *What was I thinking? What kind of dad am I? I should have let her hit me! A broken leg—a broken anything—would have been worth keeping my little girl from killing herself.*

How many times had I told myself that I would go to any length to protect my children? That I'd face anything. Take on anyone. Die, if necessary.

Yeah, right. When my child needed me most, I bailed. And the more I thought about it, the more disconsolate I became.

God, however, used that event in my life. He reminded me that even though I hadn't been there for Kiernan, He had.

God is never late. And He never backs down. He will be there, through the years, to protect my children when I'm not around.

Any ability that I have to safeguard my family is merely an illusion.

A depressing thought? Maybe. Until I realize that I'm not omnipresent, but God is. And He's the one who's been protecting my family all along. Has He given me a role to play? Yes, certainly. But the burden is His.

This thought comforts me as I watch my kids race toward adulthood. As they step into unfamiliar situations, push forward into new realms of discovery, and reach to achieve new milestones in life, I don't have to try to hold them back because of my own fear. I can trust God to extend to them the same grace that He gave me as a child. And let me tell you, that was *a lot* of grace.

ABUSING MY GUARDIAN ANGEL

There were some bushes growing next to our house when I was a kid—thick, shrubby things that reached almost to the eaves of our one-story rambler. Since my parents didn't get home until several hours after I got out of school, I was the typical latchkey kid. And those bushes paid the price for it.

To play one of our favorite games, my friends and I would climb up on the roof of the house by way of the back-yard fence. From the roof, each guy had to stand with his hands down by his sides and dive off *headfirst* into the middle of one of the big shrubs. If he stuck, he won the game. But if he fell out, he had to do it over again.

Later, we'd take turns writing our names in lighter fluid on the cement floor of the garage and lighting them up. Then we'd head out into the desert behind my house and catch scorpions to bring home and torment our sisters with.

I imagine Klaxons were going off in heaven every day around two o'clock in the afternoon: "Charlie Holton is home from school! Muster a platoon of guardian angels, on the double!" It's a testament to God's protection that I lived long enough to attend high school.

When I think about my three boys in light of my own childhood, it makes me shudder. Actually, it makes me want to encase them in large plastic bubbles so that they'll be protected as they careen around our farm like crazed pinballs.

But there's just no way.

I can't possibly protect my sons from every life-threatening situation they can find to tempt fate with! It's enough to make me think that I'll end up in a padded cell one day. Even so, God is using these stretching times to teach me that "fate" really has nothing to do with the safety of my children.

I still do what I can to protect my kids from harm, of course, but learning to trust God with their lives keeps the ulcers at bay and helps assuage my fears for their safety. I can take joy from their boyhood exploits and allow them to explore their world without hovering over their shoulders at every step. I no longer feel the need to smother my children in foam padding to keep them safe, because I know that the Almighty is their first line of protection. Any additional safety net I can provide is probably more for my own peace of mind than anything else.

This doesn't mean that I let my kids play in the street or sword-fight with each other—well, not with *real* swords, anyway. Sometimes, however, trusting God means taking risks. Or allowing my kids to do so. Or it may mean making unpopular, maybe even unreasonable, decisions. Yes, there *is* a line between trusting God and being careless or irresponsible. God gave us the capacity to sense danger, and we should use it. We should never purposefully endanger ourselves, our families, or those around us without a reasonable certainty that what we are doing is in keeping with God's will as revealed in His Word.

John Piper puts it this way:

When we risk losing face or money or life because we believe God will always help us and use our loss, in the end, to make us more glad in his glory, then it's not we who get the praise because of our courage; it's God who gets the praise because of his care. In this way risk reflects God's value, not our valor.[13]

WHAT ABOUT YOUR FAMILY?

Risking your own life, money, or plans for God's glory is one thing. But if you're anything like me, you are keenly aware that your actions affect your family as well. Should you ever put your family at risk? Isn't that irresponsible?

Once again, it depends on how you define risk. Objective risk is a function of ignorance—you do not know the outcome of your choices beforehand. This means that there's no way you can keep from making decisions that endanger your family to some extent. You really have no choice, short of locking everyone up in a castle tower and pulling up the drawbridge. (And even that has its risks.)

If, however, you define risk from a biblical perspective—risk only comes with being outside of God's will—then you do have a choice. To endanger your family in this way *would* be irresponsible. But endeavoring to keep your family in God's will may require the assumption of some objective risk. And without a proper, well-exercised faith, fear will always follow.

A careful reading of Exodus 20:5 shows that the best way to protect your children is to be obedient to God's calling in your life. The verse says, "I, the LORD your God, am a jealous

God, punishing the children for the sin of the fathers to the third and fourth generation."

To me, this means that when I disobey God, I'm not only putting myself in danger; my family is in it with me. Shrapnel in physical combat doesn't discriminate by guilt or innocence, and neither does the fallout from my spiritual failings. To me, this is a huge motivator toward obedience.

Jewell Machlan knows the cost of taking risks for the cause of Christ. In 1987, she and her husband, along with their two young sons, were serving as missionaries in Ethiopia. They had been there for over three years and Jewell was pregnant with their third child when her husband was killed in a helicopter crash. Grief-stricken and unsure what to do next, Jewell packed up her children and moved back to the States. She didn't see how she would ever be able to return to the mission field, though her passion for missions remained.

A few years later she ran into Glenn, a friend from high school. He, too, had also answered a call to foreign missions, working in Hong Kong and other areas. Jewell and Glenn hit it off, and several months later Glenn proposed. Both felt called to return to missions work when they were married in 1991.

Did Jewell have to think twice about exposing herself and her family to the potential of losing another husband and father? "Not at all," she asserts. "I loved being on the mission field, and know that is where I am supposed to be."

By the time the Machlans made it to the Philippines, they had a two-year-old daughter, and their other children were twelve, ten, and seven. The mission agency asked the family to go to the remote village of Mangali, about 260 miles north of the capital city of Manila. The journey would require a four-hour bus ride, followed by an hour-and-a-half trek by jeep to the trailhead. From there it was nineteen miles on foot to the village.

While still in Manila, Glenn met a missionary whose family had just returned from the same province. Her family had pulled up stakes after their two-year-old daughter had been stabbed by one of the villagers. The tribe they would be living with, she told Glenn, still practiced the tradition of revenge killings and periodically went to war with neighboring villages.

Glenn thought of his own children. Was it irresponsible to put their lives at risk for the sake of his calling? Would God really ask that of him?

Later that day he got word that a local man named Nelson had been pastoring alone in Mangali for some time, all the while praying that God would send someone to translate the Bible into the Tanudan Kalinga dialect. When Nelson heard that the Machlans were on the way to do just that, he had literally jumped for joy.

Glenn knew then that they were doing the right thing. "I just had to trust that God would take care of us," he says, "not by protecting us from harm, necessarily, but that His grace would be sufficient for us, no matter what happened."

Glenn and Jewell are still in Mangali to this day. While ministering to the three hundred families in the village, they have braved tribal wars, injuries, and sickness. They know they have a job to do, and God has confirmed that calling time and again. As far as the Machlans are concerned, there is no safer place they could be.

★ ★ ★

SEVEN

BULLETPROOF KIDS

Throughout history, parents have worried about their children's safety. You might say it goes with the job description.

My own informal polling suggests that one of the greatest fears that assails parents—mothers, in particular—is that of some tragedy befalling their children. When I was growing up, parents reminded their kids not to take candy from strangers, to look both ways before we crossed the street, and for Pete's sake, to stay off the roof. (Okay, maybe that last one was just something *my* folks said. I was told as a child, "Be careful—cars aren't the only thing that can be recalled by their maker.")

These days our children are taught to be afraid of nearly everything! Many of these warnings come from the media and our schools, but parents must also share in the blame. It concerns me to see how many Christians, too, have bought into this culture of fear.

Schools in our area now practice "sniper drills" along with fire drills.

A recent book called *Chemical-Free Kids* touts itself as "Your guide to the whereabouts of...invisible dangers—the toxic substances that permeate our food and environment." So apparently children's after-school snacks are also dangerous. Watch out for those Twinkies!

Some parents move to the country to escape the dangers of city living, only to lose touch with many of their friends, who will no longer bring *their* children to visit because they are concerned about the risks of living in the *country*.

It's completely natural for parents to be concerned for their children's safety. We are, after all, responsible for the little tornadoes until they move out of the house. I believe it is unhealthy, however, when we model fear to our children and teach them to be afraid of everyday things in their everyday world.

This is one reason that, several years ago, I became convinced of the necessity to model for my children a fear-free worldview. As I began to notice the fear messages bombarding my family from all sides, I knew I had my work cut out for me. Where were these messages coming from? How were they shaping the way my children perceived their world? And how could I show them how to filter that incessant input through the lenses of a biblical worldview?

ONE THING TO FEAR

On a recent trip to the public library, I found myself looking again into the pages of Ayn Rand's classic novel *Atlas Shrugged*. I'd read the whole eleven-hundred-page tome several years ago, but I wanted to find a certain passage that had particularly impressed me. Rand's book deals with two boys being taught at home, and this brief passage struck me as the perfect description of the attitude I hoped to foster in my own kids.

The scene finds the main character, Dagny Taggart, noticing how these boys were different from most children she was used to dealing with:

> She often saw them wandering down the trails of the valley—two fearless beings, aged seven and four. They seemed to face life as she had faced it. They did not have the look she had seen in the children of the outer world—a look of fear, half-secretive, half sneering, the look of a child's defense against an adult, the look of a being in the process of discovering that he is hearing lies and of learning to feel hatred. The two boys had the open, joyous, friendly confidence of kittens who do not expect to get hurt, they had an innocently natural, non-boastful sense of their own value and as innocent a trust in any stranger's ability to recognize it...certainty that life held nothing unworthy of or closed to discovery, and they looked as if, should they encounter malevolence, they would reject it contemptuously, not as dangerous, but as stupid, they would not accept it in bruised resignation as the law of existence.
>
> "They represent my particular career, Miss Taggart," said the young mother in answer to her comment. "They're the profession I've chosen to practice.... I came here in order to bring up my sons as human beings. I would not surrender them to the

educational systems devised to stunt a child's brain, to convince him that reason is impotent, that existence is an irrational chaos with which he's unable to deal, and thus reduce him to a state of chronic terror."[14]

Even though this passage was penned in 1957, and Ayn Rand was not a Christian, her words draw strong parallels to the battles that Christian parents face today.

Although homeschooling is not an option for every family, it is important no matter where our children attend school that we proactively teach them they have only one thing to fear—*life apart from God's will and purpose.* This is especially vital if our children are exposed to daily doses of fearmongering by the world, whatever the source.

Helping them to understand and appreciate the sovereignty of God over all situations will instill in our kids a wide-open optimism and fearlessness about what is to come. It will free them to risk total obedience to the Lord's calling in their lives, opening up the path of lifelong joy. As the psalmist wrote, "I run in the path of your commands, for you have set my heart free" (Psalm 119:32).

ANTIDOTE TO THE POISON

How do we counter the pervasive cultural messages that constantly remind our children to be afraid? Job number one, of course, is to conquer fear and timidity in our own lives. Then, we must learn to release our fear for our kids. Why? Because when our children perceive that we are afraid for them, they will believe there is reason to be afraid.

While it may be natural to worry about their safety, we need to constantly remind ourselves that God has a place for our children in His plan and that He will extend to them the same amount of grace, discipline, and protection that He afforded us as we grew to maturity. This is a tremendous test of faith, more difficult even than abandoning our own lives to His will.

My own mother speaks of facing this issue when I was just an infant. One night she was standing over the crib, watching me sleep, when God quietly spoke a question into her heart: *If I take him, will you still follow Me?* As hard as it was to say, she softly answered, "Yes, Sir."

Indeed, the mere fact that I survived into adulthood is a testament to God's power to save us from our own poor choices. My parents swear to this day that, practically from birth, I kept an entire platoon of guardian angels busy around the clock. I remember wanting to be a stuntman after watching Lee Majors as *The Fall Guy* on TV. My friends and I cooked up all sorts of idiotic stunts that should have landed us in the hospital, or worse. In spite of our reckless ways, however, God was faithful in protecting us—even when we were all but begging to end up in traction.

Yes, parents most certainly do have the important responsibility of safeguarding their children as they grow up. But this solemn duty must be understood in light of the fact that no matter how hard we try, our children's safety ultimately rests in *God's* hands. We should not spend time obsessing over things we cannot control, but instead, work hard to teach our children to be prudent and trust God to work out His purposes in their lives.

What I'm getting at is that *safety*, as we define it—i.e., an absence of physical or emotional injury—should not be our first priority for our children. Just as *I* would rather have a meaningful life than a long one, I need to pray first and foremost that God will lead my children into His purpose, even if that means they will face some hardship or pain along the way.

Remember how God tested Abraham, calling upon him to sacrifice his son Isaac? Once Abraham followed God's instructions without question, bound his son, and drew back the knife to kill him, an angel of the Lord called out to him, "Do not lay a hand on the boy.... Now I know that you fear God, because you have not withheld from me your son, your only son" (Genesis 22:12). Among the things the patriarch learned from this heart-wrenching encounter was that God's plan for Isaac trumped Abraham's plan for Isaac. And Abraham had to rest in the knowledge that God's plan was best.

I recently got a call from a frantic mother whom I'll call Michelle. Almost beside herself with anxiety, she was sure that her daughter, Liz, was about to ruin her life by joining the military. She wanted me to talk her daughter out of this decision.

"How old is Liz?" I asked.

"Nineteen."

I thought for a moment and said, "Then I don't see how it's my place to discourage her. Nor yours, for that matter. I'll be happy to help her understand the realities of life in the military, so that she will know what she's getting into. But if she chooses to go ahead with it, the best thing you can do is give her your support."

"Support?" Michelle wailed. "But it's a mistake!"

"Maybe. But it would *also* be a mistake for you to assume that God won't use this experience to teach Liz something—maybe something she couldn't learn any other way. If you fight her on this, and try to manipulate her into doing what *you* want her to do, it will only damage your relationship. It will also probably increase the chances that she will join for the wrong reasons.

"Besides," I continued, "did *you* ever do anything when you were her age that you came to regret?"

"Of course!"

"And God dealt with you through those mistakes, right? Didn't He use them to teach you something?"

"Well, yes."

"Then what makes you think He won't do the same for Liz?"

Michelle sighed a long sigh. "I just don't want her to go through the pain that I did."

"Then you'd rather deprive her of the chance to get closer to God through it?"

"Well, no."

This devoted mom was allowing her fear to make her lose trust in God's sovereign power to guide Liz into His purpose, just as He had done in her own life. What Michelle needed was to hand over the steering wheel of her life to God—and then encourage her daughter to do the same. If you are a parent, you know which is more difficult.

It's a knee-jerk reflex for us dads and moms to want to insulate our children from hardship. While this desire may be perfectly normal, we must be careful to avoid manipulating circumstances in an attempt to force our preferences and choices on our young adults. Yes, we are parents, but that doesn't give us the right to play God.

Don't get me wrong. I'm not saying that we should write our teenagers off, or that we shouldn't make ourselves available to counsel them on their decisions. I'm simply saying that there comes a point where we must trust God to take care of them just as He has us. When the children are younger, it is our solemn duty to safeguard them. But even then we must work to avoid becoming so fearful for their safety that it affects how we relate to them. We need to encourage our children to encounter and learn about the world with prudence and discernment, but not with the spirit of fear.

One of the best ways to achieve this balance, I believe, is to severely limit the amount of time each week that the television is on in our homes.

SHUNNING ARTIFICIAL REALITY

Carefully screening the types of shows you watch as a family is a given, but there's an even more important consideration here: We need to guard our children from the habit of engaging in passive behavior for hours each day. This includes, among other things, watching television, surfing the Web in a non-learning capacity, chatting with friends on-line, and playing video games.

I recently took a poll of the class of tenth graders I teach in Sunday school each week. To my dismay, each of these Christian teenagers spent an average of three hours a day engaged in one or more of these pastimes. That adds up to twenty-one hours a week—or the equivalent of a good part-time job. This represents more time than they spent reading, studying, praying, serving others, eating, and exercising combined. After sleeping and attending classes, it was the single largest consumer of their time.

No wonder John Piper refers to television as "the great life-waster."

In his book *Don't Waste Your Life*, he writes:

> A mind fed daily on TV diminishes. Your mind was made to know and love God. Its facility for this great calling is ruined by excessive TV. The content is so trivial and so shallow that the capacity of the...heart to feel deep emotions shrivels.[15]

Television is so unhealthy on so many levels that it's hard to know where to start. But to consider just one aspect, let's focus for a moment on how TV instills fear in us and in our children.

TV bombards us with messages warning us to be afraid. Most of these messages are fed to us with the motive of selling us something, be it face cream or tires. This may be done directly—"Don't trust your family's future to just any insurance company"—or indirectly—"Are you getting the quality you deserve?"

TV provides a breeding ground for our imaginary fears. Popular television dramas weekly spin scenarios of ever more creative and gruesome ways for people to die, fueling our imaginations in the worst possible way. Even before primetime, the nightly news alerts us to every bizarre and horrific event on the planet, from mudslides in third-world countries to flesh-eating bacteria to multicar pileups on the interstate. Few of these events have any real impact on our own lives, but they feed us a steady stream of new things to be afraid of. Even fewer of these news stories present us any opportunity to actually *do* something about the suffering being paraded before us.

All of this mayhem is interspersed with commercials for weight-loss products and sports cars, precluding any serious consideration of the tragedies just presented to us. Stir it all together and we're led into a sort of complacent passivity. We feel powerless to do anything about a world coming unraveled at the seams. And that produces anxiety and fear.

Television invites us to sin. When you get right down to it, there just isn't much on TV these days that has any redeeming value. In fact, the morals portrayed even on commercials are so shallow and counter to those of the church that the shows themselves sometimes pale in comparison. You wouldn't allow a stranger into your home who made it his business to corrupt your children—teaching them to use profane language or pursue abhorrent lifestyles—so why would you accept these things from the media?

Ultimately, however, though we may do our best to limit our children's exposure to harmful activities and dangers, the whole point of parenting is to launch our children into the wide world.

LETTING GO

Psalm 127:3–5 describes God's view of your children:

> Behold, children are a heritage from the Lord, the
> fruit of the womb a reward. As arrows are in the hand
> of a warrior, so are the children of one's youth.
> Happy, blessed, and fortunate is the man whose
> quiver is filled with them! They will not be put to
> shame when they speak with their adversaries [in
> gatherings] at the [city's] gate. (AMP)

Children as arrows in a quiver. It's an interesting word picture, powerful and deep. Children extend the reach, the impact, of a man or a woman on their world. They must be aimed well and true at the beginning of their lives to find their mark. But in order for his children, his arrows, to reach their full potential, the warrior must do one thing in particular.

Let go.

An arrow is of little use if the warrior keeps it in his hand.

Raising children requires much grace, and we must take care not to damage the relationships we have with our young men and women by allowing our fears to smother them. There must be a conscious effort to give our kids over to God's care—and it starts when they're still in diapers. We should strive to instill the attitude in our children that Jim Elliot had: *I am immortal until God is finished with me here.*

When we can give our children up to God, we pave the way for them to develop a bulletproof mindset.

PART II

PREPARING FOR BATTLE

★ ★ ★

EIGHT

A SPIRIT OF POWER

In 1944, millions of American servicemen and women headed off to join battles in Europe and the Pacific. Most were draftees with upbringings as diverse as America herself—from Cajuns and Eskimos to Wyoming farmhands and city boys from Boston. Almost none of them had any real understanding of military life before they reported for an abbreviated boot camp. Drill instructors had orders to rush these raw recruits through, to get them into units on the front lines as quickly as possible.

With this in mind, the Army published a War Department pamphlet designed to help ease the transition to military life for the new recruits. The booklet covered everything from drill and ceremony and pay to group living and military courtesy. Focusing as it did on the skills and attitudes of a good soldier, the little book brought help and encouragement to many a lonesome private away from home for the first time and uncertain of what would happen next.

As believers, we too have such a book, tucked away in the latter pages of our Bibles. Spiritual warriors—young and old, male and female—can learn from its few pages what God's soldiers should look like and how they should conduct themselves in any number of battle situations.

The book is the apostle Paul's second letter to Timothy, and in the next few chapters, we will look closely at this letter with an eye toward identifying the characteristics of a good spiritual warrior. Along the way, we'll be drawing on the battle-tested insights of an old soldier as he passes them on to a promising young recruit.

We will see that a good soldier:

- learns to control his or her fear (2 Timothy 1:7).
- gets special training for a specific mission (1:9).
- endures hardship (2:3).
- is focused—not bogged down in civilian affairs (2:4).
- vigorously pursues whatever mission he's given (2:10).
- remains prepared for anything (2:15).
- sets the example and maintains high standards (2:20).
- is willing to work behind enemy lines (3:1).
- is always preparing for the next battle (3:12).
- can compartmentalize (4:5).
- understands battlefield leverage (4:18).

A GOOD SOLDIER MASTERS FEAR

The little book of 2 Timothy is peppered with military metaphors, but for the next several pages, we will focus on what Paul says about overcoming fear. Let's begin with 2 Timothy 1:7. As with so many verses in the Bible, the more you study it, the more meaning it seems to have:

For God did not give us a spirit of timidity, but a spirit of *power*, of *love* and of *self-discipline*. (emphasis mine)

I find it interesting to note that Paul refers to fear specifically as "timidity." He doesn't seem to take issue with the *feeling* of fear, but rather with the unwillingness to carry on in spite of that feeling. Soldiers understand that when the bullets start flying, it's okay to be afraid. Feeling fear, even admitting to it, won't get you labeled a coward. Cowardice is *using* that feeling as an excuse to abandon the mission. The military understands this and so, from basic training on, soldiers are taught that fear reactions are normal and shared by everyone exposed to combat. Even though a man feels afraid, he can keep going and get the job done; in doing so, the fear will subside.

While doing research for an article a couple of years ago, I had the opportunity to interview a military psychologist attached to the 75th Ranger Regiment. I didn't remember having a resident psychologist when I belonged to that unit, and I was frankly curious about what role he played.

"So," I asked, "do you have a couch in your office where you counsel soldiers?"

"No," he laughed. "My job is more about crafting the environment soldiers live in—to help mitigate the effects of the high-stress situations they operate in."

The psychologist proceeded to lay out the strategy that he and the unit leadership had come up with, based on studies going all the way back to World War II. These time-tested methods are designed to help the Rangers overcome the stress and fear that naturally go along with their profession. It all came down to three focus points that form the crux of their program—all of which fit hand in glove with the prescription laid out in 2 Timothy 1:7.

Power. Love. Self-Discipline.

Let's take a look at each part of this formula.

KNOWLEDGE IS POWER

The military psychologist I interviewed told me that, according to special-ops leaders, the more technically and tactically proficient a soldier is, the better he'll perform when the chips are down. What's more, the power he brings to the fight will be compounded by the quality and depth of his preparedness.

It's been said of both backpacking and battle that the more you carry in your head, the less you will have to carry on your back. Preparedness casts off the burden of fear.

For instance, when a soldier sees a vehicle bearing down on him on the battlefield, his fear will quickly spike if he can't identify it. But if he's been well trained in vehicle recognition, he will quickly be able to tell if the vehicle carries friend or foe, and react accordingly. As a consequence, his fear will be diminished.

Knowledge is power because it helps the soldier perceive the reality of the battlefield correctly. Knowledge leads to understanding, and understanding to decisiveness. Decisiveness, in turn, increases the chances of victory in battle.

Special-ops officers train ceaselessly to be as proficient as possible in every aspect of warfare so that they'll be able to perceive the reality of the battlefield correctly. This is why the single greatest common denominator found among these elite warriors is *confidence*.

Confidence in their ability to perform their assigned tasks.

Confidence to endure stressful situations.

Confidence that they will overpower and defeat their opponents.

This confidence is deeply embedded in the culture of these units. The Special Forces creed—a set of principles recited by every Green Beret almost as scripture states boldly, "I will not fail those with whom I serve."

What does Paul mean when he writes that God has given us a "spirit of power"? Does it mean the Holy Spirit will come upon us as He came upon Samson, enabling us to slay Philistines with the jawbone of a donkey? What kind of power is he talking about? And how do we access it?

The more we familiarize ourselves with God's ways—understanding how his Holy Spirit enables us to obey in every circumstance—the more we can tap into that power. The more familiar we become with His Word, His will, and His ways, the easier it becomes for us to see God's hand in our lives. In that sense, knowledge *is* power.

Confidence is every bit as important in the Christian life and in spiritual warfare. We gain this steady assurance by seeing things from God's point of view. Our power comes from the applied knowledge of God's Word, His will, and His ways. This applied knowledge is also called *obedience*. Being technically and tactically proficient in God's army means not just understanding Scripture, but living it.

Understanding God's ways means learning enough about *who God is,* to know that He always has our best interests at heart and that He really is more powerful than *any* obstacle we may encounter in life. Psalm 25:10 says, "All the ways of the LORD are loving and faithful for those who keep the demands of his covenant."

THE AMAZING RACE

Every summer, for years, I have taken youth groups on wilderness survival trips. One of the most popular events of these trips is an *Amazing Race*–style event where we drive the group out into a remote corner of West Virginia to go "hiking." At some point, however, we suddenly stop by the side of the road and tell them to get out. We then hand them an envelope and drive away.

The group is bewildered. They hurriedly open the envelope, hoping to find instructions inside. Instead, they find a card with a riddle on it, something like "He watches Matt's box."

Now they're totally confused. They have no idea where they are, who Matt is, or how to find him. They've been given no instructions, rules, or guidelines. They have no clue as to their ultimate objective. An adult accompanies each team but offers no assistance.

Eventually, they begin wandering down the road until they happen upon a farmer in his field or passing by on a tractor. They flag him down and ask for help. The farmer gives them a lead on someone who might be able to help them, a person who lives down the road a few miles. Encouraged, the group starts off that way. A few minutes later, a friendly local might stop his truck and offer them a ride.

In the end, the kids find out that Matt has a small business in the valley, renting videos. He has a small video drop box that sits in the center of town, directly in front of the house of a man named Steve Wymer. Several hours later, when the team shows up at Steve's house, he is sitting on his porch, envelope in hand. Inside is yet another bewildering clue…and the process begins all over again. The teams continue finding clues until midafternoon, when all the teams end up at a finish point where they find me waiting.

That night around the campfire, we discuss the day's events. The teams describe how unsettling and scary it was to be left in an unfamiliar place, with no explanation of the game's objectives. For many of them, it was the first time they ever felt that they were operating "without a net."

What the teens didn't see that day was how I orchestrated everything that happened to them and kept tabs on their progress every step of the way.

I explain to them how the trip had been planned months in advance, how I had *arranged* for the farmer, the friendly local who offered them a ride, and Steve Wymer to be ready to play their parts in the team's journey.

We talk about how life is a lot like this. We are often confused as to our purpose and get scared because it feels like we are working without a net. And yet God is always there, behind the scenes, charting the pathway ahead of us. He carefully orchestrates everything that comes into our lives and uses it to draw us into His purpose, to lead us to the place where He wants us.

One of the most mind-boggling things about God's power and creativity is that He uses even our mistakes to further the process of making us more of who He wants us to be. Don't get me wrong, we can still disappoint Him by not following His plan, but we cannot disrupt His greater purpose. It's just that when we choose to walk in His ways, He can use even our mistakes as training for our mission. Truthfully, this is too amazing for me to fully comprehend.

As we learn more about the way God works, the uncertainty of life is pushed aside by the absolute certainty of His eternal love for us. Psalm 119:105 says, "Your word is a lamp to my feet and a light for my path." Apparently that lamp isn't meant to be bright enough to show us where the path will end, but only to illuminate the next step. When we are able to trust Him and obediently take the next small step we are shown, life stops seeming so dangerous and becomes a great adventure.

The most interesting thing about my survival weekends is that during the trip, the participants are rarely comfortable. We issue them one meal per day; they get little sleep and camp in the woods without tents or sleeping bags. They get wet. They get cold. By the middle of the second day, most of them hate me.

Yet when they get back home, they can't stop talking about the trip. By facing the challenge, the teens feel like they've accomplished something. They didn't just go camping; they left the confines of their comfort zones and learned something about themselves in the process. The next time they encounter a challenge at home or at school, the endurance they've gained from the "extreme weekend" will make their situation easier to handle.

In most cases, the kids can't wait to go again next year.

The knowledge that I am planning the trip ahead of time turns the uncertainty into adventure. And so it is with the Christian life.

Understanding God's plan gives us power. But getting to know how God works starts with the realization that His plan has more to do with making us like His Son than it has to do with making us comfortable. Unfortunately, since our culture has made comfort the be-all and end-all of existence, we tend to pick up some of that mentality.

When I was in the Army, my platoon sergeant liked to say, "If you are comfortable, something bad is about to happen." Just as with military training, spiritual training needs to be arduous and challenging because of the unforgiving nature of battle. We need to cultivate the habit of *pursuing* these challenges and not running from them. Understanding that we grow through trials will help us to understand and accept God's ways and will make us more alert to His working in our lives and the lives of others.

Hardship is always easier to bear when we understand that it has a purpose. Author Randy Alcorn once mused, "Isn't it interesting how we pray for God to make us more like Him, and the moment He puts something in our lives in order to do just that, we immediately ask Him to take it away."[16]

An elite warrior in God's army understands the payoff of joy that lies on the other side of misery. He makes a practice of not shying away from uncomfortable situations, knowing that by facing them he will be better prepared to confront and overcome the crises in his life through God's power.

On this subject William Barclay writes:

> It is not craven fear, it is courage, that the Christian service should bring to a man. It always takes courage to be a Christian, and that courage comes from the

continual consciousness of the presence of Christ. In the true Christian there is the power to cope with things, the power to shoulder the back-breaking task, the power to stand erect in the face of the shattering situation, the power to retain faith in face of the soul-searing sorrow, and the wounding disappointment. The Christian is characteristically the man who can pass the breaking point and not break.[17]

We tap into this awesome power by choosing to obey His commands and pursuing the mission that is set before us. We can best understand that mission through the knowledge of how God works and what He wants to accomplish in this world, and we get that knowledge through a study of His Word.

★ ★ ★

NINE

A SPIRIT OF LOVE

*"Greater love has no one than this, that he
lay down his life for his friends."*

JOHN 15:13

We need litter bearers! Give me some volunteers!"
Tracer rounds flashed by, inches over his head. Joe
Cicchetti pressed his body into a low concrete wall. He
turned his head to see the medic advancing down the line of
men in a crouching run. Cautiously peeking around the corner, he spotted some men from his unit crawling around a
pile of rubble that used to be a building on the other side of
what used to be the street.

At that moment, an artillery round exploded in the street
between him and the other men. He flinched instinctively at
the blast, metal fragments filling the air around him. A few
seconds later, when the momentary shock of the too-close
explosion wore off, he could hear the anguished screams of at
least two of the men he'd just been watching. Rage welled up

inside of him. In desperation he raised his rifle and fired off a few rounds in the direction of the enemy.

It was February 9, 1945, and Cicchetti would have given anything to be back home in Waynesburg, Ohio, shoveling snow, instead of fighting his way through the Philippine capital of Manila. The Japanese had converted the Manila Gas Works and several surrounding buildings into a fortified death trap for the GIs, with interlocking fields of machine gun, mortar, and heavy artillery fire. Cicchetti's unit had taken heavy casualties all day as they advanced on the enemy.

Joe could endure the fatigue of day after day of combat. He could handle the screech and crash of battle. He could even stomach the possibility that he might die in this forsaken place. But what he could not stand were the tormented cries of wounded men whom he had come to think of as brothers. The sight of them—bloody, mangled, sometimes shell-shocked and limp—was just too much.

He felt a hand on his shoulder. It was the medic, shouting above the din of the battle. "We've got more wounded than we can handle," he was saying. "Can you find some people to help carry a litter?"

Joe didn't hesitate. "I'll do it."

He found three other men and began shuttling wounded buddies back to the relative safety of the aid station. Mortars and artillery continued to fall all around, but the heartrending cries of their fallen comrades kept the team coming back, braving enemy fire again and again. At one point they became pinned down by heavy machine-gun fire. Every time they tried to move, the bullets would zing all around them.

Joe's anger returned, rising in his throat, until he could

stand it no more. "Get ready to move," he told the other three men as he unslung his rifle. "I'll draw their fire while you get past them, then I'll catch up with you." Without giving them time to protest, he said, "Go!" and got up and charged toward the bunker, zigzagging as he went.

The machine gun opened up on him like a fire hose, but he somehow avoided being hit. A moment later he worked his way around the flank of the enemy position. Then in one quick move he rose up to his full height and fired off an entire magazine into the machine-gun nest. When he was done, three Japanese gunners lay dead.

Joe turned and ran back toward the line, where he knew more injured were waiting. On the way, he spotted a group of wounded soldiers stranded behind the remains of a small building. With mortar rounds pounding their position, it was obvious they wouldn't survive there much longer. The private from Ohio took off toward them at a dead run.

At that moment, it seemed like every enemy gun in the vicinity turned on him alone, blasting away with a new level of fury. Joe, however, charged on through the deadly curtain of enemy fire. Just before he reached the wounded soldiers, a mortar shell exploded immediately behind him, hurling the private-turned-leader a good distance through the air. Immediately recovering his feet, Joe continued running, even as hot, sticky blood coursed down his neck. It felt like molten lava was pouring into his brain, but he reached the wounded men and, without hesitating, picked one of them up in a fireman's carry and began staggering the fifty yards or so back through the hail of gunfire toward safety.

Just as he reached safe cover, and with his wounded

buddy still on his shoulders, his world faded into black.

Private First Class Joseph J. Cicchetti collapsed and there, in that foreign land so far from the snowy fields of Ohio, he died. For his heroic efforts, he was posthumously awarded the Congressional Medal of Honor, the military's highest decoration for valor. He was twenty-one.[18]

SAME HEART, DIFFERENT WAR

Nearly sixty years later, another warrior, Marine Capt. Brian Chontosh, found himself leading a patrol through the small town of Ad Diwaniyah, south of Baghdad. In what seemed like a single heartbeat, his unit was hit with a coordinated attack of mortars, rocket-propelled grenades, and machine-gun fire. Chontosh knew immediately that it was a near ambush—and that he and his men were in the kill zone.

Retreat was not an option. Dying was.

But Captain Chontosh wasn't about to let that happen to his Marines. The love he felt for each of them instantly transformed into rage at those who would try to kill his men. He ordered the driver of his Humvee to plow directly into the enemy trench, and with a violence of action that came from hard training, he leaped from the vehicle and attacked the attackers until his rifle ran out of ammo. He then pulled out his pistol and continued killing the enemy until that, too, ran dry. He picked up an enemy weapon and continued fighting. Then another. Then another. When it was over, more than twenty enemy fighters were out of commission and his men were saved.

What made him do it? "Love for my men," he says

unashamedly. "When you get to know and have that bond between each other, it overrides conscious thought. There was no fear, no rational thinking…. Everything that we did to prepare ourselves…just came automatically."

That automatic reaction came from years of hard training under realistic conditions. Because Capt. Chontosh had developed a close familiarity with counter-ambush tactics, their use under fire was instinctive. His weapons became an extension of his will, his muscles remembering the correct motions because of prior repetitive action.

Stories like these raise questions in my mind. When it comes to making the ultimate sacrifice or charging into the teeth of battle, why is it that devotion, rather than politics or patriotism, is cited as a soldier's greatest motivator? Why would a man with his entire life ahead of him lay it down so willingly for a fellow soldier, even one he has only known for a short time? Why is it that horribly wounded soldiers who have been evacuated to the rear often echo the sentiment of one Marine recently hit in Fallujah, Iraq: "I want to go back. It kills me when I see the news…when I think of all my buddies back there"?

The biggest question that comes to my mind, however, is this: Could *I* ever be that brave?

BUILDING HEROES

While facing combat requires that soldiers suppress many of their natural emotional responses to fear, there is one emotion that should never be suppressed. Surprisingly, that emotion is love. That is because love, in a paradoxical way, embodies and enables all of the traits of a professional soldier. Take a look at the Army's seven core values:

1. Loyalty
2. Duty
3. Respect
4. Selfless service
5. Honor
6. Integrity
7. Personal courage

Now look at how 1 Corinthians 13:4–7 defines *love*:

> Love is patient, love is kind. It does not envy, it does not boast, it is not proud. It is not rude, it is not self-seeking, it is not easily angered, it keeps no record of wrongs. Love does not delight in evil but rejoices with the truth. It always protects, always trusts, always hopes, always perseveres.

Amazingly, the Army's list and the Lord's list fit together hand in glove.

Loyalty—is patient, keeps no record of wrongs, trusts, hopes
Duty—protects
Respect—is kind, not rude
Selfless service—is not self-seeking
Honor—is not envious, proud, or boastful
Integrity—does not delight in evil but rejoices in truth
Personal courage—is not easily angered, always perseveres

The military knows that building camaraderie (love for one's brothers-at-arms) encourages the kind of selfless sacrifice that is the hallmark of a good soldier. It has gone so far as to make this desired trait one of the tenets of the Soldier's Code, which says, in part:

No matter what situation I am in, I will never do anything for pleasure, profit, or personal safety which will disgrace my uniform, my unit, or my Country.[19]

Camaraderie is built by shared experience, shared hardship, and shared purpose. Naturally, the more hardship a unit endures together, the more tight-knit the members of that unit become.

In the case of the 75th Ranger Regiment, a full-time psychologist is employed to help tailor the unit's living and working environment in such a way as to build esprit de corps among the men. Doing so has been found to ease the stress that naturally accompanies life in this demanding military specialty.

Research has shown that by structuring the Rangers' surroundings so that they spend a large amount of time together at a small unit level, unit cohesion increases and, as a result, combat effectiveness is improved.

Ranger leaders always look for ways to remind each man that he's part of something important, something bigger than himself. These men belong to a unit that lives, eats, sleeps, trains, and fights together, and the men pride themselves on the unit's exceptionally high standards. This fosters an environment that encourages men to be not just good at what they do, but *better*. Always better. The third stanza of the Ranger Creed, memorized by every Ranger, asserts:

> Never shall I fail my comrades. I will always keep myself mentally alert, physically strong and morally straight and I will shoulder more than my share of the task whatever it may be. One hundred percent and then some.[20]

This pledge serves as a constant reminder of each Ranger's responsibility to be a standard-setter and that failure in any area of their lives reflects on the whole of the unit.

This sense of brotherhood and unity builds confidence and security in several ways. First of all, it's reassuring to know that someone will always be watching your back. And that knowledge makes you want to redouble your efforts to watch the backs of others. This means a soldier will stay in the fight for the men to his left and right, even when every cell in his body screams at him to run for his life.

This carefully crafted culture also fosters a positive peer-pressure environment within the unit. Because any man who slacks off becomes a liability to the soldiers around him, you can be sure this man's fellow soldiers will keep him accountable.

Shouldn't our churches inspire such devotion?

I recall one instance during Operation Just Cause when I noticed that one of my privates had removed his helmet. We were sitting in a forward observation post, and there was nothing happening at that moment. In fact, we hadn't seen any sign of the enemy in hours. Our Kevlar helmets were heavy and uncomfortable, made more so by the heat and humidity, which left us feeling perpetually soggy. So while lying in a shallow fighting position, this private decided to get a little more comfortable.

I immediately leaned over and growled in his ear, "Put that bucket back on your grape and leave it there. I don't care if it *is* uncomfortable. I'm the one that has to drag your carcass out of here if you get hit."

"Roger, Specialist," he said sheepishly, replacing the helmet.

In combat, comfortable will get you killed. A tight-knit unit fosters an environment where soldiers aren't afraid to remind each other to remain vigilant. Soldiers who really care for each other don't shrug their shoulders and walk away from a situation that needs attention. As a result, you end up with an accountability structure that simply can't be beat.

"WE TAKE CARE OF OUR OWN"

Soldiers understand instinctively that the actions of the others in their unit have a profound effect on their own lives. In combat, you're either an asset or a liability. There is no third option. One of Murphy's laws of combat states, "Never draw fire—it irritates everyone around you." War is hard enough without those on your own side making it even more difficult.

As God's soldiers, we must also stay alert to our need for the company of fellow believers. We need to purposefully spend time with people who will, through their words and actions, encourage us to lead a strategic life. We need to be involved in a church body that loves us enough to exert positive pressure on our lives. We need the steadying influence of believers and leaders who aren't concerned about making us comfortable, but who will challenge us to become confident, committed disciples who consistently make the tough decisions.

Being part of a group like this strengthens us to delay gratification in our lives, helping us understand the value of taking on difficult challenges. We will do it because we understand the consequences to those we love anytime we choose comfort over Christ. When we belong to a group like this, we can better understand the weight of our decisions on others—both positive and negative.

When I spend a Saturday morning with my buddies helping a single mother whose husband has left her, doing the things for her that *he* should have been doing—yardwork, auto maintenance, and spending quality time with her kids—it helps me and the other men there understand just how valuable we are as husbands and fathers, and it encourages us *never* to leave our own families in such a predicament.

When I choose to sin and disobey God in private, does it have an impact on my fellow Christian warriors? You bet it does. In the days of Joshua, one man's selfish decision brought defeat to an entire army and destruction to his family (see Joshua 7).

On the positive side, it should give us a greater sense of our own value as members of the body of Christ when we work together with our fellow soldiers toward a common goal. C. S. Lewis wrote at length about the spiritual battles that we face, likening church to a meeting of underground fighters:

This universe is at war. But [Christianity] does not think this is a war between independent powers. It thinks it is a civil war, a rebellion, and that we are living in a part of the universe occupied by the rebel....

When you go to church you are really listening-in to the secret wireless from our friends; that is why the enemy is so anxious to prevent us from going.[21]

None of us can survive the rigors of spiritual warfare without the benefit of buddies who will watch our backs. People who love us ought not be afraid to call us on the carpet whenever we begin to drift from our calling. Church should be a place where I am reminded of the value of pursuing the cause of Christ, a place where I am encouraged to be not only good, but *better*. Not just better than I was, or better than I am now, but better than I *ever could be* without the help of God and my brothers-at-arms.

I want the church I attend to be like a tight-knit army unit, with a culture where brothers and sisters who share my beliefs and sense of purpose will keep me on track—and not hesitate to let me know if I'm becoming a liability to myself, my family, or His purpose.

It's important to point out, however, that in establishing a positive peer-pressure environment, the church must heed its call to be a hospital that heals the sick and wounded—not a courtroom that judges and condemns them. The Bible refers to our enemy as "the accuser," and he has no place in the church. We call it "the sanctuary" for a reason.

A doctor gives his diagnosis of the problem for the express purpose of helping the patient get better. He doesn't assign blame for the problem (at least, not in the short term), but simply states what it is and then sets about getting it fixed. That's how our churches need to be. When a medic arrives on the battlefield, he tends to the wounded as best he can without ever saying, "This is all your fault!" (Even if it is.) The first order of business is to nurse the wounded out of danger and back into health.

THE POWER OF LOVE

Fear will make you its slave. But love breaks the fetters of fear. Fear is destructive and contagious, while love is constructive and contagious. Satan has duped our culture into believing that love is somehow unmanly. Nothing could be further from the truth. Love has the power to drive warriors like Joe Cicchetti and Brian Chontosh—and hopefully you and me—to the very heights of heroism.

And fear can never do that.

★ ★ ★

TEN

A SPIRIT OF SELF - DISCIPLINE

Four…more…miles.

Four more miles. Finish them, cross the line, and he could call himself a Ranger.

Private Cory Falde plodded miserably along in the steamy predawn of early May at Fort Benning, Georgia. Every fiber of his body screamed, *Quit!* But Falde wasn't about to give up. Not after coming this far. Not if it killed him.

Wisps of steam rose from the column of men marching in front of him, the undulating line stretching off into the darkness, illuminated only rarely whenever a passing car played its beams along the formation. Except for the *crunch-crunch-crunch* of each exhausted soldier's boots on the crushed gravel road, all was silent. The sweat-soaked camouflage fatigues clung to Cory's body like plastic wrap; his feet felt like mush inside his combat boots; and the Kevlar helmet on his head felt twice as heavy as it had when the road march began.

But it really didn't matter.

Nothing mattered except crossing that line.

He made the decision before he'd started: He was going to succeed or die trying. He'd dreamed about being a Ranger since he was eight years old, and if that wasn't enough motivation, the thought of having to face his friends and family with the news that he'd washed out was all the incentive he needed to continue…putting one painful foot…in front of the other.

FINAL EXAM

This was the last major test of the three-week Ranger selection course. This trial would separate those who would join the elite 75th Ranger Regiment from the 70+ percent who would fail. The mission? Move twelve miles in under three hours wearing full combat gear, including a forty-pound rucksack.

Not all the tests had been physical. Other ordeals in the past two weeks had been designed to assess the psychological makeup of each Ranger candidate. Their backgrounds had been checked thoroughly. Anything more serious than a routine traffic citation could get a soldier disqualified.

It was plain to see that the Army was serious about filling the Ranger regiment with only the cream of the all-male, all-volunteer crop. Of every one hundred soldiers who entered the Ranger Indoctrination Program pipeline, an average of only twenty-eight were selected on their first try. Cory Falde's class had dwindled from over 150 to less than forty—even before the dreaded road march.

Falde thought back to basic training. The first few weeks had been largely unrelated to combat—or so he'd thought. They had spent endless hours marching around the PT field, learning to walk in step, to cup their fingers when they walked, keeping head and eyes forward. They had stood at attention until he could no longer feel his legs, forbidden even to swat away the flies that seemed to have a diabolic affinity for their eyes and ears. The word *clean* had taken on entirely new meaning for him with the daily barracks inspections. Apparently, everything he and his fellow trainees had done prior to their enlistment had been wrong. Now they needed to learn how to walk, talk, dress, eat, and stand the "Army way."

What was the purpose of it all? They had called it basic *combat* training, but it was nothing like Falde thought it would be. He'd expected to be shooting his rifle and blowing things up from day one. What did the interminable inspections and learning to fold his underwear in tight 4x6-inch squares have to do with being a warrior?

But now, trudging along in a fog of agony toward a blessed finish line somewhere up ahead, he could see it. Those hundreds of small discipline exercises had built within him a foundation of mental toughness, a faculty he needed every ounce of at that moment. He had grown so much in the eighteen weeks since he first stepped off the bus at the basic training facility on Sand Hill. The fact that he could now shine his boots so well that he could see his reflection in them was less valuable than the discipline he'd developed in learning to do so.

Now he understood.

But that wasn't all.

The discipline he'd been developing gave him a sense of confidence—not only in his own abilities, but in those of the men who would serve with him. When combat did come, he knew now that he could count on the men around him to have the discipline to watch his back.

Falde rounded a corner and saw the most beautiful thing he'd seen in his life. Ranger instructors in black sweats, just up ahead, wielding clipboards and logging in each Ranger as he went by. *Only a few hundred yards to go!*

Though the military had turned out to involve much more tedium than he'd expected, learning to endure the monotony had given Falde what he'd needed to accomplish his goal. And despite his pain and exhaustion, it felt *good*.

"Good job, Falde," the Ranger instructor called out as he crossed the last few feet to the finish. And then he said the words that Cory had longed to hear since he was eight years old.

"Congratulations, Ranger."

THE DISCIPLINE THAT CONQUERS FEAR

Self-discipline is the act of choosing the difficult right over the comfortable wrong. It is the practice of controlling one's will. Recognizing the bent of human nature to follow the path of least resistance, the self-disciplined individual chooses the neglected path of the hard road. A disciplined person knows that discomfort is the stimulus for all growth. Self-discipline, then, isn't just about learning to accept discomfort, but *choosing it* for the sake of personal growth.

Self-discipline means *paddling* my canoe down life's river, not just going wherever the current takes me. It is tiring, but the effort is always worth it. I may still get somewhere without paddling, but it's sure to be a more painful ride if I bounce off every rock along the way.

Since biblical times, the military has understood that self-discipline conquers fear. Time and again, commanders and their soldiers have proven the importance of toughness training. And one of the best methods for developing self-discipline is an extremely regimented lifestyle that forces the soldier to rein in his desires and control his actions in hundreds of small ways every day. In fact, the faculty of self-discipline is so important to all branches of the service that long-standing traditions have grown up in them regarding military courtesy, drill and ceremony, and physical fitness. Each of these has, at its core, self-discipline.

Gen. George S. Patton Jr. once asserted to his men, "You cannot be disciplined in great things and indiscipline in small things. Brave undisciplined men have no chance against the discipline and valour of other men."[22] Without discipline, any army is little more than an armed mob and is more dangerous to itself than the enemy.

In the previous chapter I told the story of Capt. Chontosh, who charged into battle to protect his men. Chontosh credits his training for keeping fear at bay during those few hellish minutes of all-out combat. He was faced with a group of men who spoke the language of death and violence, and when the crisis presented itself, a courage constructed from strict self-discipline emerged. Years of toughness training helped him to react with violence of action, not fear. He found that the hours of tedious, repetitive training rendered him fluent in the language of war—and enabled him to react immediately to protect his men. His weapons became an extension of his will, his muscles re-creating the same motions that he had drilled to perfection.

But what if he hadn't?

What if Capt. Chontosh had forgone his responsibility as commander and let his men get comfortable instead of doing all that tedious training? When the battle found them, they would have been unprepared—and they may have returned home in flag-draped coffins.

As my old platoon sergeant used to say, "If you're comfortable, you're wrong." Combat is uncomfortable, the very definition of a high-stress environment. Therefore, soldiers must constantly pursue discomfort in training in order to be ready for the conflict when it arrives.

In battle there is no time to think, only to react. For this reason, our military pours millions of dollars into preparedness. But being prepared involves two facets—proficiency and perseverance. Training that focuses on self-discipline increases the latter, which is the more valuable of the two traits. The frequency and tempo of military instruction is maintained at a high level, so that when these units are faced with an actual combat situation, they will be prepared to react as they have been trained to do—without having to think about it.

Blouse your boots. Starch your shorts. Put a shine on everything. Salute. Stand at attention. All of these seemingly insignificant exercises coalesce to form a soldier who can remain calm in the face of fear. An extremely regimented lifestyle builds this kind of self-discipline into soldiers through hundreds of very small actions that, taken together, enable men to respond efficiently in combat.

There used to be a commercial for motor oil where the mechanic would say, "Pay me now or pay me later!" This is how it is with self-discipline. We *will* be disciplined, one way or another. Either we can choose the rigors of self-control, or face the alternative—punishment and consequence.

Unfortunately, real self-discipline is one of our society's rarest qualities. To put it bluntly, the world—particularly our Western world with its many comforts and luxuries—is full of wimps and pansies. To the extent that any believer can develop the habit of consistently making the hard choices, he or she will stand head and shoulders above the crowd.

Think about it. Whenever you are faced with a difficult decision, isn't the more difficult choice usually the right one? So when we make a habit of choosing the more difficult path in the small things, it makes us better prepared to do so in the things that really matter. Self-discipline is like mental muscle, and it has to be exercised if it's going to grow.

William James penned the following in the last half of the nineteenth century. Though somewhat arcane in its language, this selection from his book *Habit* contains a real nugget of wisdom on the subject of self-discipline.

Keep the faculty of effort alive in you by a little gratuitous exercise every day. That is, be systematically ascetic or heroic in little unnecessary points, do every day or two something for no other reason than that you would rather not do it, so that when the hour of dire need draws nigh, it may find you not unnerved and untrained to stand the test. Asceticism of this sort is like the insurance which a man pays on his house and goods. The tax does him no good at the time, and possibly may never bring him a return. But if the fire does come, his having paid it will be his salvation from ruin. So with the man who has daily inured himself to habits of *concentrated attention, energetic volition,* and *self denial* in unnecessary things. He will stand like a tower when everything rocks around him, and when his softer fellow mortals are winnowed like chaff in the blast.[23]

Did you get that part about insurance? People buy insurance to save themselves in the event of a calamity. It's a way of preparing for the worst. Military training isn't easy, because *combat* isn't easy. In the Rangers, we didn't train hard in order to look good or to be "in shape." We were preparing for the very real possibility of having to face a deadly crisis at a moment's notice. Our leaders did their best to make these preparations as realistic as possible so that we would be ready for the real thing when the time came.

The training wasn't so much aimed at developing us physically as it was at toughening us mentally. We lived a very rigorous and demanding schedule, even in slow times, so that we could be accustomed to going without sleep or food or rest for extended periods.

In 1944, every Army soldier was issued a war department pamphlet called *Army Life.* It detailed what a new recruit could expect from the Army—everything from pay and benefits to personal welfare and training. This manual holds some real wisdom that applies not only to soldiers of that day, but to our lives as well. On the subject of training, it says:

There is one factor more important than any other in overcoming fear. It is training. Skill, not muscle alone, makes a champion in the ring. It also makes a soldier who wins. Knowledge and training build confidence and skill. These dispel fear. You must take your training seriously. Training will make you—as an individual—able to win your fights. Give it your best. If you don't, you have the most to lose.[24]

As spiritual "light fighters," you and I face the same dangers as any other soldier. But the ambushes, attacks, and bombardments we face are spiritual in nature. It stands to reason, then, that the more spiritual training we acquire, the better prepared we will be to apply the knowledge of God's truth in defeating the adversary in our everyday lives.

This is why we should seek to develop "spiritual toughness." When the time comes that you or I find our integrity caught in a near ambush—at the sudden opportunity to profit unfairly or the accidental occasion to indulge an unhealthy passion—will our spiritual "muscle memory" be sufficient to cause us to react in a way that will spare us the pain of regret? Or will we become casualties due to poor planning and badly executed responses to the attack?

All of us fail to respond correctly at times. But the good news is that God can use these mistakes to actually make us stronger. In fact, He promises in Romans 8:28 that He can use everything we go through in life to better prepare us for our mission in His purpose.

As author James Loehr puts it, "In many ways, the storms of life nourish us and provide a foundation of personal strength for future battles. They also bring us face-to-face with our weaknesses and literally force us to get moving."[25]

It could also be said that the tough times in our life show us most keenly our constant need for God's care and kindness.

You may never plan to get into a situation where people are shooting at you. Having been there, I'd never wish that for you, either. But the truth is, everyday life can be tough enough to break anyone who is unprepared. In a spiritual sense, life is combat. That's why exercising your will by making tough choices every day is so important.

When the crisis comes, will you stand like a tower when everything rocks around you? Or will it find you unprepared? You can let yourself become a casualty, and the war will still be won without you. God's purpose will not be thwarted. The question you and I face is this: *How big a part shall I play in the winning of this war?*

William James referred to three types of self-discipline exercises: concentrated attention, energetic volition, and self-denial. What follows is a list of ideas in those three categories that I suggest incorporating into your daily and monthly routine. Adopting one of them for a month means this "gratuitous exercise" might just become a habit, and it will certainly go a long way toward building the muscles of your will. Besides, thirty days is long enough to give the feeling that you've accomplished something, yet short enough to be practical.

Keep in mind, this is not self-discipline for its own sake. First Timothy 4:8 says, "For physical training is of some value, but godliness has value for all things, holding promise for both the present life and the life to come." What I'm saying is that our physical selves are tied to our emotional and spiritual selves. Increased discipline in one area will affect all the others. Building physical discipline will make it easier for us to control our emotional urges and help us stick to the high road spiritually.

The apostle Paul draws strong parallels between physical self-discipline and spiritual fitness:

> Everyone who competes in the games goes into strict training. They do it to get a crown that will not last; but we do it to get a crown that will last forever. Therefore I do not run like a man running aimlessly; I do not fight like a man beating the air. No, I beat my body and make it my slave so that after I have preached to others, I myself will not be disqualified for the prize. (1 Corinthians 9:25–27)

"But we do it to get a crown that will last forever."

Look at that sentence. What do we do to get a crown? We go into "strict training." We prepare for the battles ahead so that our faith will stand the test when under fire. Here's a question for you: Would your lifestyle qualify as strict training? I hate to admit it, but all too often, mine does not.

With this in mind, try some of these exercises.

CONCENTRATED ATTENTION

Ask yourself, *What could I do to sharpen my mind, become more alert and discerning, and know God better?* Find little things that you can do that will increase your value as an employee, or as a spouse, or as a committed disciple of Christ, instead of simply droning in front of the television after work. Here are some suggestions.

- Memorize an entire chapter of the Bible, or better yet, a whole book. Too tough? Many Muslims memorize the entire Koran, word for word. Some of them don't even speak Arabic but memorize the sounds. Don't shortchange yourself. And don't think so small. Make a habit of leaping tall hurdles and you'll never stumble on a small one.

- Keep track of every penny you spend in a month. You'll be surprised where God's money goes. Many marriage counselors cite money matters as the number one cause of divorce. By becoming a better steward of the resources God gives you, you will experience the great blessing of becoming more effective in His service—and probably have a better marriage to boot.

- Keep a diary for a year. It will be fun and informative to look back on later, and will certainly show you how often God answers your prayers.

- Take a month and learn everything you can about another religion—or a cult such as the Jehovah's Witnesses or the Latter-Day Saints. It will help you better defend your faith when challenged, and through your study you may learn things about your own faith that you never knew.

- Decide to do something nice for someone every day for a month. This one might just change your life. Find persons at random and do them a kindness with no hope or expectation of repayment. Whether you know them or not, it makes no difference. Get a notebook and keep track of what you did and for whom. Send a thank-you note to a friend for just being there. Mow your neighbor's lawn. As you go through the drive-through for a burger, pay for the stranger's meal in the car behind you and then drive away. I guarantee this will be some of the most fun you will ever have, and more important, it will make you think outside yourself.

• Learn a new skill. Take up a hobby you've always wanted to pursue. Get out of the rut of going to work, coming home, sleeping, going to work, coming home....

• Much has been said about the value of reading the entire Bible in a year. I agree that it is a very good discipline exercise. But here's one that you may find equally rewarding: Read one book of the Bible, over and over again, every day for a month. You will find that the words' meanings get deeper and broader with every reading. New insights open up and nuances of meaning become apparent that you may never have caught before. Now you aren't just skimming the Word of God, but tasting it, mulling it over, and meditating on it.

• Spend some time researching your family tree. You may find yourself blessed, as I was, to discover the legacy of faith that exists in your ancestors. Besides, it's good to know your roots.

• Get a pen pal. I'd suggest corresponding with someone in prison. It will give you the chance to share the love of Christ with someone who needs it badly and will remind you of the consequences of sin.

ENERGETIC VOLITION

It shouldn't come as a surprise that investing energy into your life and the lives of others multiplies that energy—and multiplies the impact your life has on those around you. Physical self-discipline pays dividends on a spiritual and emotional level.

- Force yourself to do twenty-five push-ups a day. Or five, for that matter. It's the act, not the quantity, that counts. Put signs all over the house as reminders. Twenty-five push-ups a day might not do much for your body, but the simple act of disciplining yourself to do it is great exercise for your mind. Do this for a month, however, and you're sure to see improvement.

- Look into foster or respite care for a needy child. In the U.S. alone, there are over 130,000 children who don't have homes. Christians talk so much about stopping abortion, but what are we, as believers, doing about those who live? How about sacrificing a weekend a month to mentor a needy teen? Better yet, adopt one of these precious kids. If the church would step up to the plate on this issue, there wouldn't be a foster care problem in this country.

- Run a mile a day. Make it two.

- Get up a half-hour earlier each day for a month. Do something constructive with this extra time. Do it for a year and *voila!*—you have one week more to get things done than those who are still sleeping.

- Plan an expedition, not just a vacation. Do something monumental. Maybe climbing Mt. Everest is out of your reach, but find something that will give you a sense of accomplishment when completed. A few years ago, I took three days with a couple of friends and we rode our bicycles from one end of the Chesapeake & Ohio Canal to another. It's a 185-mile-long bike trail in our area that was built in the 1800s as a way to get cargo from Cumberland, Maryland, to Washington DC. By the time I finished the ride, it felt like I'd been sitting on a belt sander for three days—but I get to talk about it for the rest of my life.
- Run a marathon. Running 26.2 miles is something to be proud of, but the real accomplishment is in the discipline required to train for it.
- Choose one Saturday morning a month for a year to go help a friend work on *his* honey-do list. You will be building an important friendship—and don't be surprised if the favor is returned someday.

SELF - DENIAL

The most common form of self-denial found in the Bible is fasting—abstaining from food for a specified period of time. A fast may last anywhere from one meal to forty days. This is still a very effective self-discipline exercise with far-reaching benefits. The late Dr. Bill Bright, founder of Campus Crusade for Christ, wrote, "Fasting is the most powerful spiritual discipline of all the Christian disciplines.

Through fasting and prayer, the Holy Spirit can transform your life."[26]

People don't fast much anymore, but maybe we should. Jesus thought it was important. He fasted for forty days in the wilderness. That's hard core!

If you aren't yet ready to go without food for five weeks, try some of these less-demanding discipline exercises. The basic principle is the same: You are building the muscles of your will and strengthening your faith.

- Fast from TV for a month. You might have to get your family to try this one with you. If you do decide to withdraw from what I call "the electronic income reducer," then pack it away somewhere so no one will be tempted to turn it on. At least unplug it and turn it around or, as a last resort, hide the remote. Chances are no one in your house remembers how to turn the TV on manually. Use the time you save to get back into the habit of reading, playing games as a family, and spending time outdoors. You may find that you never want to go back to being a slave to the tube.

- Drink only water for a month. I try to do this at least one month every year, and I'm always surprised at how difficult it is. I'm also surprised (though I shouldn't be) at how much easier it is to stay awake in the afternoon when I don't drink twenty ounces of Dr. Pepper at lunch. I usually lose ten pounds or so in that month.

- Spend a weekend by yourself in complete silence. Read, pray, study, hike, whatever, but don't watch television or listen to music.
- Give up chocolate for thirty days. (Okay, I'll admit this one might be a little excessive.)
- Forgo your daily mocha grande. Take the money you would have spent and expend it frivolously on some unsuspecting soul. At the end of thirty days, I'd wager you will be more joyful than at the beginning. And the caffeine withdrawal symptoms may have subsided somewhat as well.
- Give up snacking between meals for a month. (As I write this, I'm sitting at my computer munching Jalapeño Cheez-Its.)

If you don't keep control of the easy things, the difficult ones will blow you out of the water. A man who wants to stay faithful to his wife must exercise the will to do so long before the opportunity to cheat presents itself. If he indulges his eyes at every opportunity and doesn't keep a tight reign on his thought life, he has very little chance of being able to say no when a young lady at work tries to seduce him into an affair.

Self-discipline is a means to an end, not an end in and of itself. Soldiers understand that discipline is the cornerstone of any successful military operation. The same can be said for the Spirit-led life.

Are you tapping into God's power through an intimate relationship with Him? Are you involved with a body of other believing men and women who are committed to keeping you accountable and supporting you when times get tough? Have you already decided how you will react when you find yourself in a situation where you are tempted to sin? Are you working daily, weekly, and monthly to become a more disciplined follower of Christ?

Anyone who intends to be used by God as an elite soldier in His service must first come to the realization that joy often lies on the other side of misery. So we should never shrink from the possibility of it. It is essential that all of us work to train our minds, wills, and emotions so that we can be useful to the Master.

Don't make the mistake of thinking you can overcome cowardice by yourself, however. Power, love, and self-discipline are gifts from God, and our focus must be on maintaining open lines of communication with the Commander. Only then will the power of these gifts be unleashed in our lives.

For Pvt. Cory Falde, graduation from the Ranger indoctrination program was just the beginning. Since then, he's been in combat three times and has trained with the Rangers on four continents. He's now a Ranger leader and can speak from personal experience about the importance of self-discipline in overcoming fear on the battlefield. The foundation of fitness that he's been building since basic training has served him well.

It will do the same for you.

★ ★ ★

ELEVEN

THE ELITE SOLDIER

The apostle Paul probably never set out to launch a military ministry.

As it happened, however, he found himself in close quarters with a number of Roman soldiers during the course of his career. (Too often, they were guarding him as a prisoner!)

Paul generally enjoyed a good rapport with the legionnaires (see Acts 28) and had great respect for their professionalism and dedication. Even in light of his experience with the government in general and the military in particular, Paul wrote forcefully in Romans 13:4 that the government is "God's servant to do you good." He also clearly came to consider himself a soldier in his own right (see Philemon 1:2)—a warrior for Christ, engaged in a war with eternal ramifications.

As his life drew to a close in the dark, cold confines of a dungeon in Rome, the battle-weary apostle penned his last letter—to Timothy. With perhaps a clearer understanding of the importance of his mission than ever before, Paul filled this letter with military references to encourage his young charge to continue the fight.

Like a grizzled, experienced sergeant showing the ropes to a young private, Paul lays out the characteristics of a good soldier in God's army: *I may be on my way to the executioner's block, Timothy, but they can't lay a finger on me. I'm invincible until God says my mission is over and it's time to go home. And so are you! Be bold. Be strong. Be faithful. Trust your Commander. And no matter how hard or discouraging or dangerous the Mission becomes, never, never turn back.*

FILLED WITH THE SPIRIT

"For God did not give us a spirit of timidity, but a spirit of power, of love and of self-discipline" (2 Timothy 1:7).

As we have seen, a good soldier learns how to overcome fear through the Spirit. As Christians, we've been given the Holy Spirit—who is the Spirit of truth (see John 15:26)—and when the truth resides in us, it sets us free from fear as we tap into the limitless inner enabling of the Spirit. Then we will be able to say with David, "Though an army besiege me, my heart will not fear; though war break out against me, even then will I be confident" (Psalm 27:3).

SET APART

"So do not be ashamed to testify about our Lord...who has saved us and called us to a holy life—not because of anything we have done but because of his own purpose and grace" (2 Timothy 1:8–9).

God's soldier lives a life set apart, dedicating himself to a cause larger than himself. God has a mission custom-tailored for each of us to accomplish during our short stay on earth. It is our calling to be "on mission" every day.

Our country's soldiers voluntarily give up some of their freedoms as American citizens in order to ensure that freedom for others. As Christians, we are to do the same. Paul wrote, "Though I am free and belong to no man, I make myself a slave to everyone, to win as many as possible" (1 Corinthians 9:19).

To Paul this wasn't about heroics; it was simply about fulfilling a mission. As John Piper says, it's not about our valor; it's about God's value.[27]

LONG-SUFFERING

"Endure hardship with us like a good soldier of Christ Jesus" (2 Timothy 2:3).

A good soldier understands that warfare is not comfortable, and he doesn't expect it to be so. He lives a life of purpose-filled privation, meaningful misery, and postponed payment. The soldier realizes the importance of pulling his own weight—because if he doesn't, someone else will have to.

SUBMITTED

"No one serving as a soldier gets involved in civilian affairs— he wants to please his commanding officer" (2 Timothy 2:4).

The private on the line rarely understands the big picture, but rather, trusts the intent and wisdom of his Commander. This gives the private the freedom to perform his part of any military operation. The elite warrior works in secret, happy to be a part of the solution, but equally satisfied when the glory goes to the Commander.

HELD TO A HIGHER STANDARD

"In a large house there are articles not only of gold and silver, but also of wood and clay; some are for noble purposes and some for ignoble. If a man cleanses himself from the latter, he will be an instrument for noble purposes, made holy, useful to the Master and prepared to do any good work" (2 Timothy 2:20–21).

Elite soldiers are set apart from regular units, distinguished in their dress, their actions, and their level of training and discipline. They voluntarily hold themselves to a higher standard so that they can take part in the most important missions. For the Christian soldier, Paul makes it clear that if we will "flee the evil desires of youth" (v. 22), we can be of greater use to God for His purposes.

I need the Holy Spirit's help in overcoming my flesh—in even *desiring* to overcome my sinful inclinations. But that doesn't mean I sit back on a couch cushion and passively wait for it to happen. Paul says that "if a man *cleanses himself*" from unworthy purposes, he will become a useful and productive vessel in the Lord's service. And he will be *made* holy. Only God can do that. But as we work to break with our old ways and sinful habits and cry out to God for His grace, He picks us up, cleans us out, and gives us a high purpose in His kingdom.

Even broken vessels find great use in God's hands. But He

will not use dirty vessels. A good soldier keeps himself clean.

ABOVE PETTY ARGUMENTS

"Don't have anything to do with foolish and stupid arguments, because you know they produce quarrels. And the Lord's servant must not quarrel; instead, he must be kind to everyone, able to teach, not resentful" (2 Timothy 2:23–24).

Good soldiers choose their battles wisely, refusing to be pulled into no-win confrontations for the sake of argument. The best tactics are those that allow us to win without disputing or fighting, where possible.

Don't forget that everyone has the right to be wrong. We must be careful to focus on what's truly important and not get caught up in some quixotic "global war on error." Colossians 4:5 implores us to "be wise in the way you act toward outsiders; make the most of every opportunity."

PRUDENT AND DISCERNING

"But mark this: There will be terrible times in the last days. People will be lovers of themselves, lovers of money, boastful, proud, abusive, disobedient to their parents, ungrateful, unholy, without love, unforgiving, slanderous, without self-control, brutal, not lovers of the good, treacherous, rash, conceited, lovers of pleasure rather than lovers of God—having a form of godliness but denying its power" (2 Timothy 3:1–5).

God's soldier understands the battlefield and doesn't expect his path to be strewn with sunshine and roses. He operates in hostile territory in uncertain situations, with people who cling to different worldviews. Armed with discernment from on high, he prudently and carefully avoids becoming influenced by the very ones he seeks to rescue.

AWARE

"In fact, everyone who wants to live a godly life in Christ Jesus will be persecuted" (2 Timothy 3:12).

People don't join the Army looking for a cushy, armchair job with a company car, thirty-minute coffee breaks, and a 401(k). They enlist because they want their lives to *mean* something. Yes, there are those who join up for the college benefits, and they're the ones who show up on *Oprah* whenever a war is looming. But the professional soldier never labors under the misconception that he lives in a Girl Scout camp. He *knows* war will be tough, and he prepares for it.

PREPARED

"Preach the Word; be prepared in season and out of season; correct, rebuke and encourage—with great patience and careful instruction" (2 Timothy 4:2).

A good military leader understands that the mission comes first, and how well it gets accomplished hinges on the level of preparation of his unit. For this reason, it is vital that the leader love those whom he serves, and serve those whom he loves.

FOCUSED

"But you, keep your head in all situations, endure hardship, do the work of an evangelist, discharge all the duties of your ministry" (2 Timothy 4:5).

In order to survive on the battlefield, it's important to compartmentalize and focus on the mission at hand. With a million and one things vying for our attention every day, we must strive to reduce the number of lesser commitments and eliminate the outright distractions and time-wasters from our lives. Simply turning off the television (and backing over the remote with your car, for good measure) will take you a long, long way down that road.

"The Lord will rescue me from every evil attack and will bring me safely to his heavenly kingdom. To him be glory for ever and ever" (2 Timothy 4:18).

Though he himself is lightly armed, the elite soldier is one of the most powerful forces on the battlefield. Why? Because of the awesome firepower at his command. In the battle for Afghanistan, a few special forces soldiers could take out thousands of enemy fighters with only a laser pointer, because they knew how to tap into the power of the U.S. Air Force bombers at their disposal. Some of the Northern Alliance soldiers who witnessed these battles mistakenly believed that the laser pointer itself had this incredible destructive capacity, not understanding that it was just a tool that unleashed a power from above.

Paul understood this concept well. Near the end of his letter to Timothy, he cites the real power behind his victories in battle. Paul wanted to be sure that no one mistook his actions for the faith as heroics on his part; he was simply tapping into the most powerful force in the universe—which is at our disposal as well.

May we learn to give the credit for our own successes to our Commander, as Paul did. And may we learn to be fearless warriors on the battlefield of life, through the power of the Holy Spirit who resides within us.

Time is short. The mission cannot wait. Let's get to work.

* * *

TWELVE

THE FRUSTRATED WARRIOR

0300 hours, 4 March 2002

The sound of an approaching chopper echoed through the predawn darkness blanketing Takur Ghar, a snow-covered, ten-thousand-foot peak in the remote reaches of northern Afghanistan.

Standing in the back of the MH-47E Chinook helicopter, a Special Operations Forces (SOF) reconnaissance team clung to the red nylon webbing covering the walls of the aircraft. It was no easy thing to stay balanced as they checked their gear one last time.

Petty Officer Neal Roberts, a Navy SEAL, prepared to be the first to exit the aircraft, positioning himself on the chopper's rear ramp. Outside, the snow glistened in the moonlight.

The U.S. Army had been monitoring a large pocket of Al Qaeda and Taliban forces in the area for some time, and a large military operation, code-named Operation Anaconda, had been planned to wipe them out. Part of that operation involved positioning recon elements on surrounding hilltops. These teams would assist the operation by providing intelligence and calling in supporting fire.

And that's why, in that dark hour before dawn, the big Chinook chopper with special-ops soldiers was about to set down on that lonely mountaintop.

The Chinook approached the designated LZ (landing zone) in a small saddle just below the summit of Takur Ghar. As the chopper neared the ground, the pilot spotted a scattering of goat skins—and human footprints in the snow. The mountaintop was already occupied.

He called back to the team commander, "Looks like our insertion may be compromised, sir."

"Do we have enemy contact?"

"No, sir, but there are definitely signs of recent activity here."

The special-ops pilot flared the helo to slow it down, coming to a hover over their intended landing spot.

"Roger," replied the mission commander over the Chinook's intercom. "Abort mission."

Before the pilot could acknowledge the command, something like a small meteor struck the helicopter, blazing through the aluminum skin, throwing flame and shrapnel around the cargo bay, puncturing hydraulic and fuel lines, and wounding one man. The helicopter lurched to one side as the pilot struggled to maintain control. The rear crewman slipped and plunged out the open door as a machine gun began peppering the wounded Chinook, invisible fingers of death stabbing holes in the thin exterior, looking for flesh inside.

Tethered to the aircraft with a safety harness, the rear crewman dangled only a few feet below the ramp. Reacting quickly, Petty Officer Roberts dropped to his belly and reached out to help the crewman inside. But it was clear that the helicopter wouldn't stay in the air for long, and the pilot jerked violently on the collective to try and gain some altitude in the thin mountain atmosphere. The action nearly stood the chopper on its tail, and with no safety harness to stop him, Neal Roberts slid out the rear door. His buddies watched him fall about ten feet to the snowy outcropping below.

As the Chinook pulled away from the mountain, the rest of the team watched helplessly as Roberts came under heavy enemy fire. The last they saw of him, he was returning fire, attacking a superior force and doing it all alone.

The helicopter crash-landed about seven kilometers north. An unmanned aerial vehicle was diverted to observe Takur Ghar, and it reportedly sent back video of Petty Officer Roberts fighting off the enemy for over an hour until his automatic weapon, sidearm, and grenades were completely expended. At that point, he was overrun and killed.

The tragic chain of events continued. A rescue operation mounted to retrieve Roberts' body culminated in one of the most intense firefights in the U.S. war on terror to date, resulting in the death of all the Al Qaeda and Taliban fighters on that hilltop—and six more American special operations soldiers were killed in action.[28]

When I first heard the story of Takur Ghar, a knot

formed in my gut and stayed there for weeks. Something inside me kept saying, *You should have been there!* I couldn't bear the thought of my special-ops brethren out there fighting and dying while I sat safe and comfortable back at home.

There's a war raging, and here I am sitting it out!

The thought nearly drove me crazy, occupying my mind day and night. I even went to talk to a recruiter at one point, wondering if maybe this was really God trying to tell me I had left the service too soon. But one look at my five children—not to mention the aging, out-of-shape guy in the mirror—told me that my time in the special ops had passed.

NOSTALGIA AND LONGING

Don't get me wrong, I got out of the Army because I *wanted* out. I was tired of road marches, inspections, and sleeping in mud puddles. But it wasn't long after leaving active duty that I started missing it. I'm still not completely sure what it was about the military that kept drawing me back, but I think part of it had to do with how much more complicated real life is than life in uniform.

In the Army they tell you where to go and what to do, when to get up and when to come to work. They provide for your every need. In a way, it's a very secure life. Military courtesy and protocol tell you where you stand in every situation. And being trusted with men's lives and expensive equipment is a powerful narcotic. In addition, the military is an organization so much bigger than me—I can get caught up and swept along in its driving purpose. It's not all guns and glory, but the boredom and misery fade over time, leaving a somewhat unrealistic memory of that life.

As I've traveled around the country speaking over the past few years, I've found it interesting that I'm not the only one feeling this frustration. Like me, many patriotic Americans would like to be *over there,* lending a hand to the kids in uniform—no matter how unlikely the prospect. In fact, I have yet to meet a man who didn't wish he could have been a soldier when the war on terror broke out.

Why is that? Why do we have this driving sense of *ought* when it comes to watching the fight rage without us? Why do men, in particular, long to be nineteen again, fighting alongside the good guys?

I think that inside every man (and boy) there's a heart that wants desperately to right the wrongs of the world, to tough it out in a battle between right and wrong and help the good guys win. I believe God puts that warrior heart in a man's chest for a reason. Maybe it's to spur us on to be men of action in Christ's kingdom, righting wrongs and rescuing those who need to be saved.

Recently, I heard from a brother Ranger who read one of my books. Forced to leave the military after a severe injury, he has never found peace in the comfort and security of civilian life:

I felt so very useless as our brothers deployed for Afghanistan and Iraq. As much as my chosen career provides very prosperous opportunities, it is not a life of fast-roping from a hovering helicopter, making a midnight parachute jump, firing live ammunition into targets within meters of your best friends, or hearing the snapping sound of live rounds passing by you as your comrades cover your movement. I miss the adventure, the fellowship, the risk, and the challenge. I feel as if part of me is empty, never knowing if I have what it takes to meet my enemy on the field of battle and defeat him; to never know if I would pass the test of combat.

When I die there are certain things I hope for. First and foremost, I want to be able to kneel before God to have Him say, "Well done, My good and faithful servant." Secondly, I want to know that I made a difference in the lives of others and that I was a good husband, father, and friend. Lastly, *I want to know that I lived a courageous and valiant life, that I faced my enemy and defeated him in battle; that I stood in the gap for those who could not stand for themselves.* Do you understand?

Boy, do I understand. And from what I've seen, so do many, many other frustrated warriors around the country. But what to do about it?

NEVER SHRINK BACK

The easy choice would be to sit out the spiritual battles and watch from the sidelines. We could try to stifle that warrior heart and live out the rest of our earthly days in comfort. Just lay down our arms and surrender to the safety of a mediocre life.

Just recently, the Lord impressed upon me a New Testament passage I'd never spent much time with before:

Do not throw away your confidence; it will be richly rewarded. You need to persevere so that when you have done the will of God, you will receive what he has promised. For in just a very little while, "He who is coming will come and will not delay. But my righteous one will live by faith. And if he shrinks back, I will not be pleased with him." But we are not of those who shrink back and are destroyed, but of those who believe and are saved. (Hebrews 10:35–39)

"But we are not of those who shrink back."

Yes! That's where I want to be, among those who *refuse* to shrink back from their duty before God—whether or not they're wearing a helmet and desert camouflage.

So I've decided to pursue this simple course: I will surrender all the plans that I had for my life and—to the best of my understanding—follow His lead.

Wherever. Whenever. However.

The most surprising benefit that comes from this act of surrender is *freedom*. I am free to allow God into the minutiae of my life, to let Him have the bills, the career decisions, the investments, the relationships. When I pledge myself to His purpose, suddenly I know where I stand in every situation.

With Him at my back.

I must, however, rededicate myself to this choice almost daily—and sometimes even more when those nagging anxieties of an uncertain future flit through my thoughts. It's a decision I need to come back to when the crushing weight of a thousand little urgencies in my life makes me forget my greater purpose. It feels a little like agreeing to let go of the steering wheel while you're driving down the highway. Yeah, that kind of scary. But it certainly adds a modicum of adventure to my deskbound life.

DEFINITION OF SUCCESS

I ran into a good friend about a year ago, and we started talking. He seemed really down. When I asked why, he admitted he had been depressed for some time because he felt like he had never succeeded at anything. He had tried out for the Navy SEALs and missed out with an injury. Later, he decided to become an ATF agent and, shortly after making it, injured his back so severely that he spent over a year on convalescent leave. Eventually, he lost that job because of his back condition. Now my friend had hit bottom, drowning in self-loathing and self-pity.

"Chuck, why can't I just succeed at one thing? *One thing!*"

He pointed to my becoming a Ranger and said he'd be satisfied if he had just one success like that to look back on and be proud of.

Not coincidentally, I had recently been struggling with similar issues. As I looked back on my life, full of successes from the military to the business world, it had become abundantly clear to me that *none* of these attainments were due to my own savvy, physical prowess, good judgment, or tactical business skill. In fact, it was easy to see in retrospect that many of my successes had come *in spite* of stupid things I had done which, by all rights, should have ruined me. There was no way my accomplishments could be attributed to anything or anyone but God.

There were even times when I found myself sort of nettled at Him, saying, "You get the glory for everything! Why can't You just share a little bit of it? Why can't there be just *one thing* that I can call my own—*one thing* I can really be proud of?"

God, however, shares His glory with no one. And I was no exception.

My friend was stunned as I related my own feelings. He couldn't believe that, with all my accomplishments, none of them filled that gaping hole in the ego like he thought they would. Even if he had been able to become a Navy SEAL, would he be able to take credit for it?

Not if he was being honest. As a Christian, he would know, in the deep places of his heart, that God deserves *all* the glory.

In that knowledge, I finally found something to be proud of.

If I boast in anything, it is in the fact that God loves me just the same, no matter how successful or unsuccessful I am. I can be proud, not because of who I am, but because of *whose* I am.

A soldier follows orders. That's his job. Even the ones that are confusing, dangerous, or seemingly useless. As soldiers of Christ, it is our duty, as the Ranger Creed says, to "shoulder more than my share of the task, whatever it may be, one hundred percent and then some." It could be that the most important thing I will ever do has nothing to do with me personally but, instead, concerns what kind of men I will make of my three boys. (Or women of my girls!) Maybe my entire life is simply meant to act as a springboard for the next John Piper, Billy Graham, or Max Lucado.

It's a sobering thought.

People sometimes ask me if I want my boys to grow up to be Rangers. I've decided that if I can raise them to be godly men, then God can make out of them whatever He wants.

I have a hunch that most of us share the unspoken anxiety that God will take us somewhere we don't want to go and leave us longer than we want to stay. Or maybe the fear that we'll fall into the tank somehow and get ourselves into a mess He won't rescue us from. Even so...

"We are not of those who shrink back and are destroyed."

I wonder what those men were thinking when they went in to retrieve the body of their fallen comrade from that enemy-infested mountaintop in that cold and forsaken wilderness. It must have felt like the loneliest mountaintop in the world. I marvel at the courage those warriors displayed, not knowing if they would even be alive in half an hour—putting their lives, their futures at stake to recover the dead body of a brother.

Was there fear? No doubt.

Apprehension? Sure.

But none of them hesitated. And neither should we.

"But we are not of those who shrink back and are destroyed."

Until the Lord says it's time to join Him at that great marriage feast in the heavens, until He checks off the last day of the last month of the calendar of our lives...we are bulletproof.

Count me in, Lord. Let's do it.

* * *

WHEN FEAR
TAKES A BACKSEAT

0200 hours, 16 January 1998

What is a life worth?

The question hung in the back of Capt. Ted LeFeuvre's mind as he wrestled the controls of the pitching helicopter. Even in the teeth of the freezing gale-force wind pouring into the cockpit from the open cargo door, his body was drenched from exertion. His only visual reference point on that black night was the collection of floating saltwater flares that the crew of his U.S. Coast Guard rescue chopper had been able to drop around the four desperate men in the roiling sea. Clad in sodden survival suits that kept them alive, and afloat in over four thousand feet of deadly-cold water off the coast of Alaska, the men couldn't last much longer.

As a twenty-three-year veteran Coast Guard pilot, Capt. LeFeuvre had been in some tough situations. But he'd never seen anything like this. Something inside kept telling him that this mission was too dangerous. They were insane to be out here at all, much less hovering just above the waves, attempting a rescue.

The flares rose and fell precipitously, as each monster wave thundered past like a seven-story building beneath them. Furious wind gusts whipped the tops of each wave into a froth of blinding spray. For the man at the controls, sky and sea had merged into a black-on-black freezing nightmare until it was impossible to tell the two apart. The pilot concentrated all his flagging energies on keeping the Coast Guard H-60 Jayhawk above the red pinpoints of the rising and plunging flares.

Weary beyond memory, he had moments when he couldn't remember just what it was he was supposed to be doing. They'd been hovering for more than two hours, trying desperately to get the rescue basket down to the four surviving members of the fishing vessel *La Conte*, which had gone down after engine failure in rough seas off the southern coast of Alaska. By this time, the men had been floating in their survival suits for almost eight hours, the forty-degree water taking its toll on them even through the suits. The rescue chopper and its crew from Sitka were their only hope of survival. If LeFeuvre and his men gave up, the men in the water were dead. It was as simple as that.

But if we keep this up, we'll likely lose the men in the water anyway—as well as our crew and aircraft.

It was the captain's call. Was he taking too much risk?
What is a life worth?

Suddenly LeFeuvre thought his eyes were playing tricks on him. The flares rose up before him, soaring higher and higher, but didn't fall back as usual. In fact, they kept rising until they left his field of vision at the upper edge of the rain-drenched windscreen. It was as if they had flown away, and for a moment, in the fog of exhaustion that covered his mind, the sight simply didn't compute.

"Altitude! Altitude! Altitude!"

The scream of the flight engineer in his headset, who was at that moment hanging out of the side door of the aircraft, shocked him back to alertness. He was looking forward at an immense wall of water bearing down on them, a freak wave that towered above the already huge waves they had been dealing with. The urgency in his crewman's voice jerked LeFeuvre's eyes to the radar altimeter on the instrument panel. It was dropping at an alarming rate. Seventy-five feet. Seventy. Sixty-five. Sixty...

He pulled the cyclic up to the stops—calling on every ounce of the Jayhawk's four-thousand-shaft horsepower and praying it was enough to break free of the downdraft from the monster wave trying to swallow them whole.

But they were still dropping.

Fifty feet. Forty-five. Forty...

Alarms shrilled and warning lights lit up the cockpit as LeFeuvre grappled frantically with the controls. The altimeter stopped at thirty-five feet, but the black ten-story wave still bore down on them.

He could feel it coming.

So this is it. This is how I'm going to die. His mind choked on the thought. Several years earlier, another helicopter from Sitka had hit such a wave, killing all aboard.

Father, I'm ready to meet You, but do I have to die cold and wet? If there was one thing Ted LeFeuvre had always hated, it was being cold and wet.

They faced the encroaching superwave for what seemed like an eternity, the tortured whine of the engines competing with the screaming storm, the aircraft climbing almost vertically up the face of the wall of water. Then the crest of the huge roller passed beneath them—and the downdraft suddenly became an updraft howling up the back side of the wave.

And now, the four-thousand-shaft horsepower was *way* too much.

The helicopter hurtled skyward as if it had been shot out of a cannon. By the time the pilots regained control, they were six hundred feet off the sea, and three-quarters of a mile away from the four souls in the water.

What is a life worth?

At the Coast Guard's beginnings, its lifesaving motto had been "You have to go out, but you don't have to come back." Over the years, the motto had fallen out of official favor. Pilots like LeFeuvre also had their crew and their aircraft to consider. Two crews had already tried and failed to rescue the men they were now trying to pluck from the black chaos below. Would anyone blame them if they called it a lost cause and pointed the chopper home? As he thought about what had just happened with the rogue wave, though, LeFeuvre understood clearly that it had only been by the grace of God that they had been spared.

And there had to be a reason.

The pilots glanced at each other, then at the two flight mechanics and rescue swimmer in the back of the helicopter. The captain spoke over the intercom. "What do you think, boys, should we try this again?" The men were exhausted and cold, but their answer was unanimous.

"Let's do it."

Capt. LeFeuvre felt a little warmer as he powered the chopper back to the beleaguered survivors. Maybe the old motto hadn't changed so much after all.

Down in the dark, wind-whipped sea, the survivors were invisible but for the occasional flash of the reflective tape on their survival suits. Ted knew that they had been immersed now for over six hours and that their chances of survival were waning by the minute. They had to get these men aboard soon.

Trying, failing, and trying again, they finally managed to drop the rescue basket within feet of the survivors.

"I think I saw someone get in the basket!" the flight engineer shouted. He hit the *up* button on the winch and began lifting the basket out of the sea. As it neared the open door, it became clear that there was, indeed, someone inside the basket. When he tried to pull it inside, however, it seemed to be hung up on something. The engineer pulled harder and still the basket wouldn't budge. With one last pull, it finally came inside. At that second, however, the engineer made a horrifying discovery. In a flash, he realized what had made his task so difficult. A second man, who had evidently been clinging to the outside of the basket, was falling away from the helicopter, back toward the boiling black sea below. They were over one hundred feet from the surface.

There was no time to contemplate the second man's fate. The rescue swimmer and backup flight engineer on board began tending to the man in the basket, and the pilots maneuvered the helicopter into position for another try at those still alive in the water.

Learning from their previous attempts, they soon had two more men in the helicopter. The only man left was the one who had fallen. As LeFeuvre hovered over the man's body, it was clear that he had not survived the fall. With his chopper low on fuel, LeFeuvre made the decision to return to shore, where medical personnel stood by to receive the three survivors.

The crew closed the doors to the howling wind, and the helicopter flew directly to the hospital at Yakutat.

When Capt. LeFeuvre thinks back on that terrible January storm, he can't help but be amazed that anyone survived the near-suicidal rescue operation. There is no question in his mind, however, that God was there with him, in control despite the raging tempest, giving him both the will and the wherewithal to complete his mission. He will never forget the fear, but on that wild and stormy night, fear took a backseat to the force of purpose. It gave him a sense of being in God's plan at that moment in time. And with that realization, in spite of the wind and water, Ted LeFeuvre was invincible in every way that mattered.

Coastguardsmen brave stormy seas to save those who are drowning. These brave men and women demonstrate that only two things separate the rescuer from the victim: preparedness and purpose. Both victim and rescuer share the same circumstances, the same dangers. One, however, is focused on survival, and the other on servanthood. And therein lies the difference.

The rescuer goes into the stressful situation willingly,

driven by the desire to accomplish the rescue. Aided and enabled by his focused training and useful equipment, he plunges into storms and dark, dangerous waters to complete the mission.

Courage, remember, isn't something you are. It's something you do. The power to be courageous comes from good training and an outward-focused heart. When I become preoccupied with my own safety, my own well-being, I become a victim. When I work to save others, I become a rescuer. That doesn't change just my circumstances; it changes my perspective. I find happiness by leading others to it.

Another old tradition: Coastguardsmen used to use the term "souls on board" when reporting numbers of passengers on a vessel. Maybe they were onto something.

Ted LeFeuvre is carrying on a tradition of saving both lives and souls that was passed down to him by missionary grandparents and his great-great-grandfather, William Booth, the founder of the Salvation Army.

What is a life worth?

Maybe that's the wrong question to ask. Perhaps we should ask, "What is a *soul* worth?" Christ put himself on the line to save our souls from an eternity apart from Him. He threw down His life for them, then called us to do the same for others. He threw down His life and became our rescuer.

By all worldly standards, that's a risky proposition. It isn't safe. It isn't comfortable. But God apparently believes that souls are worth saving, even at the cost of great personal discomfort, or even death. And one day when we stand in His presence, we will know how much we *could* have accomplished for eternity—if only we'd taken the risk.

Like Capt. LeFeuvre, we have a decision to make. Plunge into the uncertainty, step into the unknown of His purpose, move out with the confidence that you're bulletproof until the day He intends to call you home...or live with the knowledge of what might have been.

To me, that's a no-brainer.

Story Behind the Book

In October 2002, a sniper began shooting people at random in the area where I live. The community ground to a near standstill, with people refusing to leave their homes, drive the streets, or send their children to school until the killer was apprehended.

Beyond the terrible loss of innocent victims, what disturbed me most was the reaction of many of my fellow Christians. So many seemed to cower in fear, a reaction no different from that of their unsaved neighbors. At the time, I felt that the believers in my region had passed up an unprecedented opportunity. We, of all people, ought to have modeled the peace that passes all understanding in the midst of admittedly frightening circumstances.

Over and over again, the Bible urges God's children not to be afraid. A simple walk of faith and trust in the living God yields a courageous, confident life that will draw people out of fear and darkness like a city on a hill.

To contact Chuck Holton, you can e-mail him at: chuck@bulletproofbook.com

NOTES

★ ★ ★

1. Manda Roten, "Elliotts remembered for laughter, smiles, hearts as big as the needs," *International Mission Board,* March 29, 2004, http://www.imb.org/core/story.asp?LanguageID=1709&StoryID=1436 (accessed December 14, 2004).

2. Ibid. (accessed December 14, 2004).

3. Ibid. (accessed December 14, 2004).

4. David and Naomi Shibley, *The Smoke of a Thousand Villages: And Other Stories of Real Life Heroes of the Faith* (Nashville, TN: Thomas Nelson, 1989), 12.

5. Aristotle, definition of *confidence,* http://spot.colorado.edu/~hauserg/ArEmotList.htm (accessed December 14, 2004).

6. Peter Menzel, Charles C. Mann, and Paul Kennedy, *Material World: A Global Family Portrait* (San Francisco: Sierra Club Books, 1995), 28, 236.

7. Randy Alcorn, *The Treasure Principle* (Sisters, OR: Multnomah Publishers, 2002), 33.

8. David G. Myers, "Do we fear the right things?" http://www.davidmyers.org/fears/ (accessed December 14, 2004).

9. The Heidelburg catechism, http://www.reformed.org documents/heidelberg.html (accessed December 14, 2004).

10. From a sermon by Al Meredith, Wedgwood Baptist Church, Fort Worth, TX, October 25, 2003.

11. Barry Glassner, *The Culture of Fear: Why Americans Are Afraid of the Wrong Things* (New York: Basic Books, 2000), xxiii.

12. From a sermon by Dr. Ray Pritchard, Calvary Memorial Church, Oak Park, IL, September 19, 1999.

13. John Piper, *Don't Waste Your Life* (Wheaton, IL: Crossway Books, 2003), 90.

14. Ayn Rand, *Atlas Shrugged* (New York: Signet Books, 1957), 719–20.

15. Piper, *Don't Waste Your Life*, 120.

16. From the opening-night speech Randy Alcorn gave at the 2003 Mount Hermon Christian Writers Conference, Mount Hermon, CA.

17. William Barclay, *The Daily Study Bible* (Philadelphia, PA: Westminster Press, 1960), 166.

18. PFC Joseph J. Cicchetti, recipient of the Congressional Medal of Honor, http://ww2archives.net/servlet/Template?_Template=person.html&country=usa&pe_id=213&country_name=United+States (accessed December 14, 2004).

19. Soldier's Code, http://basic.armystudyguide.com/general/soldiers_code.htm (accessed December 14, 2004).

20. Ranger Creed, http://www.benning.army.mil/rtb/RANGER/pam/creed_rgrorders.htm (accessed December 14, 2004).

21. C. S. Lewis, *Mere Christianity* (New York: HarperCollins, 1952), 45–46.

22. General George S. Patton Jr., http://www.military-quotes.com/Patton.htm (accessed December 14, 2004).

23. William James, *Habit* (Whitefish, MT: Kessinger Publishing, 2003), as quoted in William J. Bennett, *The*

Moral Compass (New York: Simon and Schuster, 1995), 239–40.

24. War Department Pamphlet 21-13, *Army Life* (Washington DC: United States Government Printing Office, 1944), 9.

25. James Loehr, *Stress for Success* (New York: Three Rivers Press, 1997), 147.

26. Bill Bright, Campus Crusade for Christ, "Why you should fast," www.billbright.com/howtofast/ (accessed December 14, 2004).

27. Piper, *Don't Waste Your Life*, 90.

28. Takur Ghar story, http://www.armyranger.com/mod.php?mod=userpage&page_id=70 (accessed December 14, 2004).

STUDY GUIDE

★ ★ ★

The following is a series of devotional studies intended to help you put into practice the precepts of this book. This study can be used during your personal devotional time or in a supportive group setting.

The format is taken from the *Ranger Handbook*'s methodology on briefing a mission. Ranger candidates learn to brief their patrols using this tried-and-true method:

- *Situation*—the overall concept of the mission (in this case, the chapter) and why it is important.
- *Mission*—a clear, concise description of the purpose of the mission; in other words, the focus of this chapter and how it applies to you.
- *Execution*—suggestions for accomplishing the mission in your life.
- *Command and signal*—resources available from headquarters. This includes a Bible verse for you to memorize and contemplate as you proceed with the mission.
- *Service and support*—an encouraging quote or thought that will motivate you to get to work.

★ ★ ★

CHAPTER ONE
SPIRIT WARRIORS

SITUATION

Most people expend the few precious moments they are given on earth in search of comfort, unaware of the spiritual war that rages around us. It's time to get on mission.

MISSION

Today, you will take stock of your life. Ask yourself the questions below and write down your answers.

EXECUTION

After writing out your answers to these questions, put the list in your Bible and look back on it from time to time.

- Am I settling for too little?
- Is fear of the unknown holding me back?
- What meaningless pursuits occupy too much of my life?
- Considering the war at hand, how could I better use that time?
- What one thing would I do with my life if I knew I could not fail?
- How do I want to be remembered when I am gone?

COMMAND AND SIGNAL

Read 1 Corinthians 15, with special emphasis on the verse below. How does this relate to developing a bulletproof mindset? How do we obtain victory over death? And having obtained that victory, what are we then charged to do with our time here on earth?

For the perishable must clothe itself with the imperishable, and the mortal with immortality. (1 Corinthians 15:53)

SERVICE AND SUPPORT

"What manner of person should he who has God with him be? In such company it behooves me to put on courage and, like Moses, go in unto Pharaoh without fear." —C. H. Spurgeon, "A Man Without Fear," from *Faith's Checkbook*

"When a nation calls its prime men to battle, homes are broken, weeping sweethearts say their good-byes, businesses are closed, college careers are wrecked, factories are refitted for wartime production, rationing and discomforts are accepted, all for war. Can we do less for the greatest fight that this world has ever known outside of the cross, this end-time siege on sanity, morality, and spirituality?" —Leonard Ravenhill

★ ★ ★

CHAPTER TWO
WHAT IS "SAFE"?

SITUATION

We live in a world paralyzed by risk-intolerance. As a believer, do you buy into the culture of fear?

MISSION

Develop a right perspective on risk.

EXECUTION

Define *danger*. Now try to answer these questions:

1. Which is more likely to cause accidental death, firearms or poisoning?
2. Which is more dangerous, road rage or your kitchen floor?
3. Which has killed more people in the U.S. in the last decade, the Ebola virus or falling soft drink machines?
4. What is the number one killer in America?

Now consider these questions:

- How do our perceptions of danger differ from the reality?
- Where were you on September 11, 2001? Do you remember what you were feeling that day?

- Do you feel safer today than you did then? Why? Are we safer today?
- Define *safety* from a biblical perspective.

The correct answers:

1. Poisoning is the number two accidental killer of people ages 18–49. Number one is car accidents.
2. Falls kill more than eight thousand people each year in the U.S. alone. Road rage results in about thirty deaths a year.
3. Falling soft drink machines have killed more than forty people since 1990. There have been no recorded deaths from Ebola in the United States.
4. Time. It eventually kills us all.

COMMAND AND SIGNAL

Therefore put on the full armor of God, so that when the day of evil comes, you may be able to stand your ground, and after you have done everything, to stand. (Ephesians 6:13)

SERVICE AND SUPPORT

"When people become very fearful they go into an altered state of awareness or functioning. The Army instills certain things in us to overcome the fear factor. One is training. If you've been trained over and over again it helps you go into overdrive, where you react out of training. All those issues of fear that come in and block your train of thought are pushed aside because of the training. Likewise, if you aren't trained spiritually, keeping your armor on, you are going to get eaten alive." —Capt. Scott C. Crossfield, chaplain who in 2002 participated in a combat aerial assault into Afghanistan

★ ★ ★
CHAPTER THREE
WHOM SHALL I FEAR?

SITUATION
When Adam and Eve chose their way instead of God's, God loved them enough to allow them to do so, but they didn't like the outcome. We, too, have been given free will, and though God's grace often pulls our chestnuts out of the fire, so to speak, it's important to remember the potential consequences of our actions.

MISSION
Count the cost.

EXECUTION
Discuss the potential consequences of *not* following God's purpose for your life. Make a list to help you count the cost of sin, perhaps focusing on one of these areas:

- Not being a good steward of your time, money, or health.
- Being unfaithful to your spouse.
- Not keeping a tight rein on your thoughts or words.
- Putting your comfort ahead of His commands.

For discussion: How can being uncomfortable keep you safe? How can the easy way be dangerous? How can a proper fear of God keep us safe?

COMMAND AND SIGNAL

Your commands make me wiser than my enemies, for they are ever with me. (Psalm 119:98)

The angel of the LORD encamps around those who fear him, and he delivers them. (Psalm 34:7)

SERVICE AND SUPPORT

"We've lost a lot of fear with God. We have made him so comfortable that we don't have what Moses was talking about in Deuteronomy 9:19 when he said, 'I feared the anger and wrath of the LORD.' We serve such a generous and gracious God that it's easy to become overly familiar and overstep our bounds. It's sort of like when I play around with my kids, yet sometimes they forget where the boundaries are. They have to learn that you can play with your dad, but there are certain points of respect, and you don't cross that line." —Gary Thomas, author of *Authentic Faith: The Power of a Fire-Tested Life*; from an article by Lynne M. Thompson, "Fearless," *New Man* magazine, September/October 2002

* * *

CHAPTER FOUR
RETHINKING RISK

SITUATION

The world (and some preachers on TV) will try to convince you that you deserve the best of everything. A new car. A bigger house. A younger wife. Our culture is obsessed with "getting mine." Ask the average person how much "enough" is, and the answer will almost always boil down to this: "A little bit more."

But what do we *really* deserve? And would getting more make us more fulfilled?

MISSION

Get off the "gimme" train. Get outside yourself. Demonstrate servant leadership.

EXECUTION

Answer these questions:

1. Name three ways the world sends the message, "You deserve more stuff."
2. Is there something inside of us that is *meant* to want a better life? Is this a godly quality?
3. How can material things increase fear in our lives?
4. Define the term "true riches." Now consider your life. How *wealthy* are you?
5. If God called you to give up all your stuff, could you do it?

This week, ask God to show you specific ways to share your wealth. Also, get rid of something in your life that is causing you fear.

COMMAND AND SIGNAL

"Whoever can be trusted with very little can also be trusted with much, and whoever is dishonest with very little will also be dishonest with much. So if you have not been trustworthy in handling worldly wealth, who will trust you with true riches?" (Luke 16:10–11)

Whoever loves money never has money enough. (Ecclesiastes 5:10)

SERVICE AND SUPPORT

"Every item we buy is one more thing to think about, talk about, clean, repair, rearrange, fret over, and replace when it goes bad." —Randy Alcorn, *The Treasure Principle*

* * *

CHAPTER FIVE

IN THE MOMENT OF CRISIS

SITUATION

Spiritual warfare sometimes spills over into the physical realm. While our battles are often best fought on our knees, there are times when we can take ground from the enemy by getting involved in places where God is working around us. Fortunately, He uses all of our past experiences as training to prepare us for these opportunities.

MISSION

Run to the guns! Find ways to get involved in what God is doing around you.

EXECUTION

Consider these questions:

1. Reflect on some of the worst experiences of your life. Can you see ways that God might use these events to prepare you for future service?
2. How is the death of a Christian different from the death of an unbeliever?
3. What are some ways that spiritual battles may become physical?
4. What can we do in our everyday lives to combat the enemy?

5. Read Numbers 13–14. How did Caleb's perspective alter his perception of the Israelites' circumstances? How does this apply to your life?
6. How should your beliefs affect your perspective?
7. The last time you encountered one of life's trials, did you act in step with your beliefs?

COMMAND AND SIGNAL

"For my thoughts are not your thoughts, neither are your ways my ways," declares the LORD. "As the heavens are higher than the earth, so are my ways higher than your ways and my thoughts than your thoughts." (Isaiah 55:8–9)

And we know that in all things God works for the good of those who love him, who have been called according to his purpose. (Romans 8:28)

SERVICE AND SUPPORT

"Christians are an exclusive subculture of confidence and calm [in] a world of relativism and ensuing panic. I'm told that the shooter, as he was coming in, was cursing God and Christians and particularly Baptists. Somebody said [that] he said, "You Baptists think you know it all." No, we don't know it all. But we do know this: 'My hope is built on nothing less than Jesus' blood and righteousness. I dare not trust the sweetest frame, but wholly lean on Jesus' name. On Christ the solid rock I stand, all other ground is

sinking sand. All other ground is sinking sand.'" —
Al Meredith, pastor, Wedgwood Baptist Church;
from his sermon given the Sunday after the
Wedgwood shootings

★ ★ ★

CHAPTER SIX

NO SAFER PLACE

SITUATION

We tend to cling tightly to those things that are most important to us. It can be much more difficult to trust God's
dominion over the lives of our loved ones than it is to surrender our own lives to Him. This is often the cause of
tremendous anxiety, especially for parents. It's difficult to
send our loved ones into a hostile environment, and some
people simply can't bring themselves to do it. But when we
learn to give the most important things in our lives to God,
everyone wins.

MISSION

Expose the fear factors in your life.

EXECUTION

Answer these questions:

1. Identify a time when you clearly saw God's protection in your life.

2. Contemplate the freedom that comes with giving charge of our most treasured possessions to God.

3. List some ways that parents could be overprotective with their children. Where is the line? How does someone fulfill their duty to safeguard their loved ones while still giving them the freedom to mess up?

4. What is the best way to teach my children to be safe? (Hint: Read Psalm 34 and Proverbs 2:11.)

5. If God said of your family, "If I take them, are you still with Me?" how would you answer?

COMMAND AND SIGNAL

Do not forsake wisdom, and she will protect you; love her, and she will watch over you. (Proverbs 4:6)

"Leave your orphans; I will protect their lives. Your widows too can trust in me." (Jeremiah 49:11)

SERVICE AND SUPPORT

"The most important thing that parents can teach their children is how to get along without them."
—Frank A. Clark

★ ★ ★

CHAPTER SEVEN

BULLETPROOF KIDS

SITUATION

The war rages on and the enemy is targeting your children. We are charged with both modeling a correct combat posture for our children and with training them to be warriors in their own right. But a soldier doesn't learn how to fight by lying about the barracks. Training must be tough, realistic, and continuous. The battle *will* reach your children sooner or later. When the time comes, will they be prepared?

MISSION

Let your arrows fly. Prepare your children to impact the world.

EXECUTION

Consider these questions:

1. How can overprotective parents damage their children's battle-readiness?
2. Can you recall the reaction of a child to the terrorist attacks on 9/11? How would you help a child to cope with a similar tragedy today?
3. How can you ascertain the readiness of a child to take on a new level of spiritual challenge?
4. What are your wishes for your children's lives? Do you wish them an easy, comfortable life? Or would you rather they experience a challenging, meaningful one?

...so that you, your children and their children after them may fear the LORD your God as long as you live by keeping all his decrees and commands that I give you, and so that you may enjoy long life. (Deuteronomy 6:2)

Blessed is the man who fears the LORD, who finds great delight in his commands. His children will be mighty in the land; the generation of the upright will be blessed. Wealth and riches are in his house, and his righteousness endures forever. (Psalm 112:1–3)

SERVICE AND SUPPORT

"I believe that in our culture today we are often more concerned about the material success of our children than we are about their spiritual success. We ought to be praying for a battlefield mentality, a mission mindset. That is our biblical role as parents. We're to be raising spiritual missiles to have an impact in our culture." — Dennis Rainey, "Trusting God with Your Child in a Non-Christian Environment," www.familylife.com

"Today there is a crying need for loving and wise men in positions of leadership demonstrating to millions of little boys and young men (who have grown up with abdicating or absentee fathers) that the Household of Faith still has fathers who govern that household with tenderness and courage, keeping watch over the souls God has placed under their charge as men who must give an account." —Tim Bayly, "Where Have All the Fathers Gone?" *Journal for Biblical Manhood and Womanhood*

* * *

CHAPTER EIGHT

A SPIRIT OF POWER

SITUATION

"As a newly inducted soldier, you will find it necessary to make a complete readjustment of your previous habits of life. You have become a part of a huge organization in which you will live in intimate daily association with other soldiers conforming to the exacting requirements of the military team. The necessary disciplinary control and the military surroundings will present an entirely new order of life for you, all essential to our great purpose in this war." —Gen. George C. Marshall, Army chief of staff, 1944

MISSION

Prepare for action!

EXECUTION

Consider these questions:

1. What is a "strategic" lifestyle? How does it differ from a civilian mindset?
2. Define *timidity*. How is it different from being scared?
3. Is fear keeping you from taking action in some area of your life?
4. Memorize 2 Timothy 1:7.

COMMAND AND SIGNAL

Therefore, prepare your minds for action; be self-controlled; set your hope fully on the grace to be given you when Jesus Christ is revealed. As obedient children, do not conform to the evil desires you had when you lived in ignorance. But just as he who called you is holy, so be holy in all you do; for it is written: "Be holy, because I am holy." (1 Peter 1:13–16)

SERVICE AND SUPPORT

"There is one factor more important than any other in overcoming fear. It is training. Knowledge and training build confidence and skill. These dispel fear. You must take your training seriously. Training will make you—as an individual—able to win your fights. Give it your best. If you don't, you have the most to lose." —War Department Pamphlet 21-13, *Army Life*, 1944

"Gallantly will I show the world that I am a specially selected and well trained soldier. My courtesy to superior officers, neatness of dress and care of equipment shall set the example for others to follow." —Fourth stanza of the Ranger Creed

* * *

CHAPTER NINE

A SPIRIT OF LOVE

SITUATION

When men find themselves in a situation where bullets are flying, one feeling more than any other keeps them there: love for their brothers-at-arms. Unfortunately, too few Christians have made the effort to seek out and nurture these kinds of no-holds-barred relationships with other believers. Why is this? Is it just too tough enduring the hardship required to form these kinds of bonds with fellow believers?

MISSION

Seek out challenging friendships by participating in a group that exerts positive peer pressure on your life.

EXECUTION

Consider these questions:

1. Why is love such a powerful emotion?
2. What keeps people from forming challenging friendships in today's culture?

3. What kinds of burdens are carried by the brethren? By the unsaved?
4. What are some meaningful ways we can share in each others' lives to cement the bonds of brotherhood between us?

COMMAND AND SIGNAL

Carry each other's burdens, and in this way you will fulfill the law of Christ. (Galatians 6:2)

SERVICE AND SUPPORT

"I'd cut off my left arm to be back with my Marines." —Gunnery Sgt. Bill Hale, wounded in Nasiriyah, Iraq, March 25, 2003

"I'm prepared to go back to my unit. We're like family." —Sgt. Christopher Nelson, shot down in a helicopter over Iraq, November 2, 2003; he suffered a broken ankle and six of his buddies were killed

"If I had one good eye left, I'd be banging on the Army's door, asking them to let me back in." —Sgt. Jeremy Feldbusch, who lost both eyes in a mortar attack on Haditha Dam in western Iraq

"I had to hobble around, but I could still shoot. I didn't want to leave my buddies." —Lance Corp. William D. Reckner, shot in the knee in Baghdad, August 10, 2003

★ ★ ★

CHAPTER TEN
A SPIRIT OF SELF-DISCIPLINE

SITUATION

"We live in the Information Age, with its emphasis on knowledge. Today, a man is judged by what he knows, rather than what he is. Therefore, men of character are rare. However, God is more concerned with what we are, rather than what we do or know. We must not only know the Bible but must also be doers of the Word (see James 1:22). We cannot be doers of the Word, especially as it concerns our life, unless we are self-disciplined. A simple definition of Christian self-discipline is the ability to stay away from sin and to do the things that please God." — Pastor Paul Choo, from a sermon, May 28, 2000

MISSION

Institute a regimen for spiritual fitness in our lives.

EXECUTION

Make a list of New Year's resolutions. Make one resolution in each of these five areas:

- *Spiritual.* How would you like to grow in the next year spiritually? Where do you need the most improvement?

- *Family.* How could you improve your family relationships in the next twelve months?
- *Physical.* Institute a fitness plan and make it a priority!
- *Academic.* What books would you like to read? What skill could you learn?
- *Financial.* Focus on what you will give, not what you will earn.

Consider this: What is the link between discipline and morale?

COMMAND AND SIGNAL

Everyone who competes in the games goes into strict training. They do it to get a crown that will not last; but we do it to get a crown that will last forever. Therefore I do not run like a man running aimlessly; I do not fight like a man beating the air. No, I beat my body and make it my slave so that after I have preached to others, I myself will not be disqualified for the prize. (1 Corinthians 9:25–27)

SERVICE AND SUPPORT

"Morale is the product of just being a good soldier. As you share experiences and hardships with other soldiers, you earn the right to that quiet pride which is part of every fighting man's personal strength. This is a pride which comes of having gotten through, when the going was tough. You feel it when you realize that you are sacrificing a great deal emotionally in becoming a soldier, and perhaps just as much materially. You show it by making that sacrifice in good spirit. Morale is knowing that what you arc doing is worthwhile. It is studying the manuals when your time is your own; staying in formation when your every muscle aches; going up into the lines when your every instinct says, "Go back!" Morale isn't just feeling good, it's what you learn the hard way." —War Department Pamphlet 21-13, *Army Life*, 1944

★ ★ ★

CHAPTER ELEVEN
THE ELITE SOLDIER

SITUATION

"There is more mental comfort, more personal satisfaction, in knowing your place and your part in this Army than in any other single thing you can now do for yourself. Be selfish about it, if you like; learn your job because knowing how to handle yourself will make you feel better." —War Department Pamphlet 21-13, Army Life, 1944

MISSION

Understand the expectations for a soldier in God's army.

EXECUTION

Answer these questions:

1. Why is simplicity a virtue for a soldier? How does this apply to your life?
2. Which verses in 2 Timothy deal with the concept of authority? How does the ability to follow orders relate to effective leadership?
3. Which verses deal with humility? How will this trait help a person become a better soldier?

COMMAND AND SIGNAL

But you, man of God, flee from all this, and pursue righteousness, godliness, faith, love, endurance and gentleness. Fight the good fight of the faith. (1 Timothy 6:11–12)

SERVICE AND SUPPORT

"The soldier whose life is on the line, who's told to go do things that are often frightening and dangerous, doesn't even get the luxury of deciding whether he's going to do it. He's told, 'Do it,' and he goes off and does it. I never met a guy out there dodging bullets or sweating in the middle of a mortar attack who thought he was in control of his life. Later he might talk about it. Earlier he might think it. But at the time, there's no doubt in his mind it's absolutely out of his hands." — Lt. Colonel Tom Hemingway, USMC (Ret.)

★ ★ ★

CHAPTER TWELVE

THE FRUSTRATED WARRIOR

SITUATION

The war on terror rages overseas. Good men and women put their lives on the line daily, taking the fight to the enemy's home turf and making themselves targets daily so that the rest of us may live in peace. But many of us feel guilty doing so and experience a sense of *ought*, as in, "I ought to be there, assisting in the fight." But do you recognize the spiritual war that is going on around you? Or are you blissfully ignorant?

MISSION

Identify the spiritual battlefields in your life. Find an outlet for your warrior heart.

EXECUTION

Consider these questions:

1. Do you ever feel frustrated with your life? Do you feel like there should be *more?*
2. Is there something inside us that's *meant* to want a better life? Is this a godly trait?
3. Would you rather have a long and comfortable life or a short and meaningful one?
4. What are the most pressing spiritual battles in your life?
5. What ways can you "get in the fight" spiritually?

This week, list the most pressing spiritual battles you face. Are they in the area of relationships? Selfishness? Priorities? Do a word search through the Bible on each of the issues you've listed. The search function on www.biblegateway.com is a good place to do this. Find a Scripture that pertains to each issue and write it down. Post it somewhere conspicuous in your home. Ask God to help you get "on mission" for Christ. Look for ways to get in the battle.

COMMAND AND SIGNAL

Everyone who wants to live a godly life in Christ Jesus will be persecuted. (2 Timothy 3:12)

...and how from infancy you have known the holy Scriptures, which are able to make you wise for salvation through faith in Christ Jesus. All Scripture is God-breathed and is useful for teaching, rebuking, correcting and training in righteousness, so that the man of God may be thoroughly equipped for every good work. (2 Timothy 3:15–17)

SERVICE AND SUPPORT

"Having armor and weapons is a far cry from being prepared to win the battle. Our weapons are spiritual, and we must be trained to war after the spirit, not after the flesh. We must be trained to wield the sword of God's warfare with skill and daring. We can be assured that our enemy and his soldiers will come at us to cripple or destroy us if possible. Lest we should be frozen with fear at this possibility, we must remember that we are not alone and that we do not have to face the enemy alone. Even though we live in enemy territory, we are not helplessly stranded. Our captain, the most skillful and successful warrior in the history of the world, is with us. He is more than willing to teach us to fight skillfully and successfully against our enemy and his forces. Yielding ourselves to His command, we can learn not only to fight for the faith and hold our own, but actually to take ground from the enemy." —Kenneth V. Ryland, "Basic Training in Spiritual Warfare," www.biblestudy.org

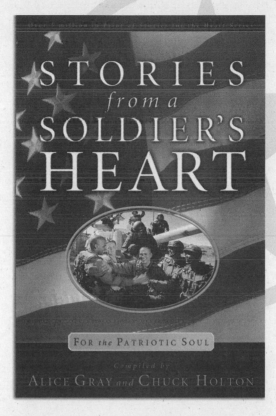

To preserve our peace of mind and our way of life, the men and women of the United States military often sacrifice their youth—and sometimes even their lives. They steadfastly guard the futures of millions of people they will never meet. Now more than seventy-five riveting stories—organized in six themed sections of patriotism, inspiration, faith on the frontlines, love and family, honor and sacrifice, and dedication and courage—bring to life these heroes and the loved ones for whom they have fought. *Stories from a Soldier's Heart* honors those who carry in their warrior hearts the world's hope for freedom.

Stories from a Soldier's Heart
Compiled by Alice Gray and Chuck Holton
ISBN 1-59052-307-5 • $12.99 US